one year...

250,000 EGGS

Bacon 6,240 lbs

660 GALLONS Buttermilk
Orange Juice 880 gallons

Sour Cream 900 lbs

3,120 lbs Butter

Hashbrowns 15,000 lbs — **900 gallons Half and Half**

432 lbs gorgonzola

12,000 oranges

Breakfast at Morning Glory: Recipes, Mishaps and Adventures from the Little Blue House by Patty Groth,
Copyright 2018,
ISBN: 978-0-692-17355-8
Printed in the USA by Bang Printing; 600 Technology Dr. Palmdale, CA 93551
www.morninggloryrestaurant.net

O'Hare Airport, Chicago

Somewhere between Boston and Oregon

Dave, why is the hood open?

Then I remembered the chair on the side of the road, and I said "Dave, we've got to go pick up that chair!" and we did just that. Somehow, we had to secure the lounge chair to the truck, so we went to a car supply shop and picked up a strap. It was at this time that Dave informed me that the gas gauge didn't work, and I contemplated buying a small gas can, but then didn't.

We slit some holes into the back of the chair and tied the chair to the inside of the truck! Now I had to learn how to drive the truck. The clutch was so tight, and the truck was loud. I was petrified! I also quickly realized that 10 days would not be long enough to drive across the country.

So, to make a long story short; I got pulled over while Dave was teaching me how to drive it and the cop forgot to give me back my driver's license, I got lost in Boston trying to get to Michael, we got detained in Canada (that's a whole other story!), we drove it as far as Chicago, flew Dave in from Boston, flew out from Chicago and let Dave finish the journey!

Dave ran out of gas more than once, not understanding the vast terrain of the west, and the lack of gas stations. It took him about a week to arrive. A month later my driver's license showed up in the mail.

The truck is sitting at Morning Glory, unfinished.

Gratitude

Where do I begin to express the immense feeling of gratitude for the most amazing people in my life, whom have helped me along the way. I would not be where I am today, without all of your help.

I start with my parents Pat and Bill Groth, who taught me how to manage life and the value of working hard, but living a full life at the same time.

My son, Adrian William Groth-Accetta, who had to endure a childhood that included his mom working a lot. My biggest joy was volunteering in his classrooms, were I would set up a mini cooking station, to teach his classes how to cook. Adrian was for years, a part of Morning Glory, bussing and prepping. I am so grateful that he has found his own path in this world. His passion is the outdoors and the medical field. (My dad would be so proud.) He is currently a mountain guide on Mt. Shasta and also enrolling in nursing school, with the intent of working for Mercy flights.

Mama and Adrian

Phil Accetta- the father of my son. Thank you so much Phil for being such a wonderful father to our son and supporting me in my Morning Glory endeavor. You were there every step of the way.

Bob Sampson- I love telling this story about you and me. We met in the halls of the CIA, in the first week of school. My new friend Hilary Hyde (we were both from Colorado), stopped me in the hallway, to introduce me to Bob, who was also from Colorado. Hilary said, "Hey Patty, this is Bob and he is also from Boulder." I looked at him and said "Oh, so you are a flat-lander! (me, being a mountain girl) and he quickly replied "and you are a Rocky Mountain bitch!" We became fast friends after that, and years later he helped me open Morning Glory! We have traveled all over the world together. I love you Bob!

Patty and Bob on top of Mount Kilimanjaro wearing our CIA hats.

Laney D'Aquino- When we are out in public together, I always refer to Laney as, "the real Morning Glory!" She has beautifully painted our iconic murals, helped designed our menues, painted our sign, put up with me, and has been my all around epic, graphic artist for the cookbook. Laney deserves a medal.

Diana von Welanetz-Wentworth: Thank you so much for believing in me. I would have never finished this book, without your encouragement and hard work. You gave me the push, that I needed, (16 years!) You have also been such a phenomenal source of expertise, soul searching, and editing, editing, editing! What a gift it has been to meet and work with you and Ted (her amazing husband!) I am so blessed and grateful.

In loving memory of Toki Cavener, who was my amazing food photographer and dear friend. We Love You, Toki!

Nick O'Connor, my Buddhist monk- bookkeeper. I call him my "Bunk!" Nick saved me from the depths of hell in my first year and he has been with me ever since. It is not always easy working for Patty Groth, and he has always done it with so much patience and grace. We would not be in business if it weren't for Nick. Thank you so much, Nick!

Lisa Shapiro: my BFF, my confidant and all around helper. You have been so helpful, on so many occasions and you have shown me what a true friend really is.

My staff: Thank you so much for working so hard. What a journey it has been! I am only one part of this giant picture and you provide the rest. I could not do this without you. Thank you from the bottom of my heart!

Much thanks and love to my sister's, Nancy and Susan.

INDEX

A
Apple Compote 146
Anthony Bourdain, may you rest in peace. What an inspiration, and so real! When his book "Kitchen Confidential" came out, it truly was, the first insider book into the realities of what it is like to work in a restaurant. He also went to The Culinary Institute of America, my alma mater, (This just happened yesterday and it shook the whole world and mine.)
Almonds, Toasted, Marionberry
   Cheesecake French Toast 62
   Tandoori Tofu Scramble 90
Amaretto Hazelnut Butter 132

B
Banana Bran Hazelnut Muffin 22
Basil Pesto 139
Beef Short Rib Hash 92
Berry,
   Blueberry Muffin 18
   Marionberry Coffeecake 28
   Syrup 144
Beverages,
   Chipotle Bloody Mary 120
   Glory-Rita 121
   Orange Cremesicle 122
   Raspberry Mojito 123
   Tequila Sunrise 123
   "The Morning After"
     Bloody Mary 120
Biscuit, Orange Cream 30
Bitch, that's me sometimes!
Black Beans, Huevos
   Rancheros 110
Black Forest Ham, Benedict 106
Blintzes, Cheese 70
Buckwheat Banana Pancakes 40
Buttermilk Cakes or Waffles 52

C
Caramelized Onion, Tofu Scramble 145
Cheddar Grits 148
Cheese Blintz 70
Chipotle Bloody Mary 120
Chipotle Lime Hollandaise Sauce 142
Chipotle, Orange Hollandaise
   Sauce 142
Chorizo, Corn Hash 94
Crispy White Cheddar Polenta 148
Cilantro Cream 134
Coconut Almond Waffle 58
Coconut Cheesecake Stuffed French
   Toast 68
Coffeecake, Pecan Streusel 28
Corn, Chorizo Hash 94
Crepes, Cheese Blintzes 70

D
Dark Cherry Syrup 144

E
Eggs Benedict 106
Eggs Creole 108

F
Feta Cheese, Tofu Scramble 88
Fresh Horseradish Cream,
   Short Rib Hash 92
French Toast:
   Coconut Cheesecake 68
   Lemon Ricotta 66
   Marionberry Cheesecake 62
   Nutella Cheesecake 64
French Toast 101 60

G
Gingerbread Waffle 54
Goat Cheese, Swiss Chard
   Scramble 86
Gorgonzola Mushroom Cream
   Sauce 141
Grits, Cheddar 148

H
Hazelnut,
   Amaretto Butter 132
   Banana Bran Muffin 22
Huevos Rancheros 100

I I want to scream right now!

J Jump for joy!
   The book is almost done!

K Kale, Risotto Cakes 104

L
Lemon Butter 132
Lemon Ginger Muffin 20
Lemon Poppyseed Waffle 50
Lemon Ricotta French Toast 66
Lemon Sun-Dried Cherry Scone 26
Linguisa Sausage, Eggs Creole 108

M
Macadamia Nut, Coconut Cheesecake
   French Toast 68
Mango Syrup 144
Marionberry Coffeecake 28
Marionberry Cheesecake French
   Toast 62
Marionberry Syrup 144
Masa Corn Cakes 102
Morning Glory Berry Muffin 18
Mushroom Gorgonzola Cream
   Sauce 141
Mushroom, Pepper-Seared Tri-Tip
   Omelet 80

"Wow!" the customers say when they first glimpse their heaping plates. Cell phones and flashing cameras appear throughout the restaurant to capture the steam still rising.

I am at my most rapt attention when Patty ladles beaten eggs into skillets to produce the best omelets anywhere. Even though I have personally demonstrated the art of the omelet to a thousand students in audiences around the world, I am eager to learn from her. Twenty containers of fillings are streamlined along the back counter so she needn't bend, and Patty's flow is one of perfection and precision as she folds the perfectly cooked eggs around twice as much filling as other restaurants!

An hour into my observation, I notice tears well up several times as I realize what it is about Patty that touches me so. This beautiful, playful woman embodies the stamina and resiliency of the generous women who have influenced me most—my grandmother who loved running a boarding house and gathering her tenants around the table, my Mom who read cookbooks like novels and loved to plan menus for parties she would never give—my own early career with my late husband Paul as cookbook authors, cooking school proprietors and early television chefs. I see in her my finest qualities, my most nurturing and devoted self.

I feel truly lucky to be perched here now as an observer because I fell in love with Morning Glory two years ago when local artist Suzanne Etienne and her husband Bob invited Ted and me to a meal that would become a revelation. Suzanne's joyful and primitive paintings fill the walls at Morning Glory, and Morning Glory became the standard to which we compare all breakfast restaurants we visit. None have come close to the vibrancy, the ambiance and the imaginative menu.

Whimsical coffee mugs for lattes, hearts crafted in foam. Salted Caramel Syrup drizzled over Banana French Toast. Sweet and tangy Caramelized Onions, house-smoked Salmon and Smoked Tomato Chutney. Oatmeal Pancakes with Walnut Butter. And everyone's very favorite Crispy Kale Risotto Cakes with Mushroom Gorgonzola Sauce. How I wish I could eat here every day!

"This woman needs to write a cookbook. I told Ted. "Everyone who comes here will want one!"

When we met, Patty and I felt instant warmth and connection. "Twins of other mothers," we decided. She confessed she had been working on a cookbook for fifteen years but was stuck and just couldn't finish it. I offered to help, and so here I am for ten days to advise, confer and write this foreword. Her dream of creating an artful cookbook, brimming with stories and photographs and the visual warmth and feel of her very personal journey is coming true!

Early years in Barrington, Illinois.
I am the one in the red dress.

Christmas 1962

My parents met at the Northern Trust Company in Chicago, with my father being a recent Princeton and Northwestern University law graduate and my mother, a secretary. They married, built a beautiful home in Barrington, Illnois and had three daughters, Nancy, Patty and Susan.
I was in the middle.

Sierra Club Trip

I was born in Evanston, Illinois and raised into a family that lived and breathed the outdoors. Fishing, camping and backpacking were under my belt by the age of four. Our heritage was mostly Bohemian and Swedish and the first settlers came in the 1860's to Minnesota and Illinois.

Cascade Mountains 1963

adventure
family
explore

In 1964,
we moved to Mill Valley,
just over the Golden Gate Bridge
from San Francisco and most
weekends we would pack up
our quintessential baby blue
Plymouth Valient convertible
and head for the outdoors.
Back then there were no
seatbelts, and we three girls
would many times, sit on top
of the backseat with the top
down!

Patty, Susan and Nancy

I loved to play restaurant with the neighborhood kids and we had a real menu from the iconic Ernie's in San Francisco, which had been designed by our neighbor, Jerry Berman, a famous graphic artist.

This is a photo of me holding up my kid's menu from Sam's in Tiburon, age 8.

Childhood Memories

My parents were "foodies" long before the current food rage. Dinner every night was something to look forward to, and my mother would pour over recipes and the magazine's *Sunset* or *Gourmet* looking for something new. We three girls had to assist my mother with dinner preparation, each taking a turn. Of course, it was our favorite chore versus setting the table or washing the dishes, and she set me on my way for a lifelong love of cooking. We always called my father the "back seat cook", as he would sit there drinking his martini and giving out orders as to how things should be done.

My father purchased for my mother a cookbook called *Culinary Classics and Improvisations* by Michael Fields. This book became her backbone (and mine as well) and she accomplished every recipe in that book. I was so excited when years later I found a used copy, for my own. We loved watching Julia Child's cooking show, but my favorite was *The Galloping Gourmet* with Graham Kerr, as he seemed to have a lot more fun.

If you were to ask me what the most influential cookbooks were for me, I would list them in this order: *Culinary Classics and Improvisations* by Michael fields, *American Cookery* by James Beard and *American Food, The Gastronomy Story* by Evan Jones.

My mother bought very few canned items, but one of them was Campbell's corned beef hash, which my father adored. Sometimes, late at night, I would hear him rustling around in the kitchen and he would be there making crusty corned beef hash with poached eggs and ketchup, and I would join him.

I loved to sit on the couch in our family room and look at my mother's cookbooks. She had a copy of *The Four Seasons Cookbook* which was from the renowned New York restaurant. I was 14 and had decided that I was going to make "Torte Sorrano" for our Christmas dinner from the *Four Season's Cookbook*. It was challenging to say the least. I had to make puff pastry, which literally took me two days to make, as you have to fold and turn dough, and roll in cold butter, many times. I ran my mother all over Mill Valley looking for ingredients like praline paste, Amaretto cookies, bitter chocolate and Maraschino Liqueur, all of which wasn't readily available, because it was 1975. I don't remember the results, because I got so sick with a terrible flu! I never got out of bed that Christmas day, so I never tasted the "Torte Sorrano."

Josh   Chip

Sandy

JoJo   Ally

Employees Behaving Badly

One cook was a closet alcoholic, and he jumped out of the bathroom window, apparently quitting. I think using the back door would have been easier! We found hidden empty beer bottles for months afterward.

Bev arrived to find one of our cooks passed out on top of our deep freezer. It provided the perfect landing for his 6' 4" frame.

I once had to turn around mid-flight on Christmas Eve, on my way to San Diego, because a cook walked out. It was busy and he couldn't handle the stress. I now get traveler's insurance.

It was New Year's eve and I was supposed to have New Year's day off. Knowing that one of my cook's would be partying that night, I offered to cook for him and he declined. New Year's day at 10am, I get the frantic call. "Patty, come quick! We are packed and all of the food is coming out burnt." I raced down to the restaurant, and there is my cook, completely wasted. I rarely get angry, but the explatives started "Get the **** out! You're fired!" I had to threaten to call the police to get him to leave. "I'll be back tomorrow", he said. "No, you will not!", I replied. I almost had a heart attack that day. I ended up hiring him back 6 months later.

One employee thought that it would be funny to plant fresh crab meat in the men's bathroom, near the hot water pipes. The stench was horrific. It took us days to figure out what was going on. He quit soon after. And it wasn't until after he was gone, that we figured out who was the culprit.

CONTENTS

Glorious Baked Goods 16

Cakes, Waffles and French Toast 36

Eggs and Others 76

Beverages 118

The Finishing Touches 130

Glorious Baked Goods

Glorious Baked Goods

Morning Glory Berry Muffins   18
Lemon Ginger Muffins   20
Banana Bran Hazelnut Muffins   22
Pumpkin Oat Nut Muffins   24
Lemon Sun Dried Cherry Scone   26
Marionberry Pecan Streusel Coffeecake   28
Orange Cream Biscuit   30

Morning Glory Berry Muffin

These muffins are our signature muffin. They are extremely versatile, moist and tender. Just change the berry, add some orange or lemon zest and you have a taste sensation. Some other variation ideas: lemon raspberry, orange blueberry or even coconut pineapple.

makes one dozen

Ingredients

1 1/2 sticks butter, softened
1 cup sugar
5 eggs
3 3/4 cups flour
1 Tablespoon vanilla
2 cups buttermilk
1 1/2 teaspoon baking soda, sifted
2 cups fresh or frozen berries
2 Tablespoons flour

1. In a mixer, using a paddle, beat butter and sugar until soft and creamy. Add eggs, one at a time, mixing well and scraping down the sides. Add vanilla.

2. Combine flour and sifted baking soda.

3. Add alternately with the buttermilk, stopping the machine and scraping down the sides until all is incorporated.

4. Dredge the berries in the 2 Tablespoons of flour and gently fold into the batter.
Do not over mix or the berries will bleed.

5. Line a muffin tin with paper cups and spray with nonstick spray.

6. Using an ice cream scoop, add one full scoop of batter to each paper cup.

7. Bake at 350 degrees for 20- 25 minutes.

Lemon Ginger Muffins

These delicate muffins are super moist and lemony but it is the fresh ginger that gives them a powerful punch. These are an easier version of a muffin that we served at Bridgecreek years ago.

makes 12 muffins

Ingredients

1 1/2 sticks butter, softened
2 cups sugar
2 Tablespoons grated lemon zest
2 Tablespoons peeled, fresh ginger, minced
5 large eggs
3 3/4 cups all purpose flour
1 1/2 teaspoons baking soda
1 cup lemon juice
1 cup buttermilk

Lemon Glaze
1 cup sugar
1 cup lemon juice

1. For the glaze, combine the lemon juice and sugar in a saucepan. Bring to a boil, then turn the heat down and reduce until syrupy, about 10 minutes. Set aside.

1. For the muffins, cream the butter and sugar together in a mixer. Beat in lemon zest and ginger.

2. With mixer on low speed, add eggs one at a time, scraping down the sides frequently.

3. Combine 1 cup each lemon juice and buttermilk.

4. In a separate bowl, sift together flour and baking soda.

5. Alternately add these wet and dry ingredients to the mixer bowl, beating until just incorporated.

6. Line a muffin tin with paper cups and spray each cup with nonstick spray. Using an ice cream scoop, add one full scoop of batter to each paper cup. Bake at 450 degrees for 20 to 25 minutes.

7. Brush muffins with Lemon Glaze while hot.

Banana Bran Hazelnut Muffins

makes 12 muffins

Ingredients

1 stick butter, softened
1 1/2 cups sugar
2 cups bananas, peeled and mashed
2 eggs
2 1/4 cups buttermilk
1 1/4 Tablespoons baking soda
3 3/4 cups flour
3 cups whole-wheat bran
1 1/2 cups brewed coffee
1 cup toasted, skinned, chopped hazelnuts

1. Line a muffin tin with paper cups and spray each cup with nonstick spray.

2. In a mixer, cream together butter and sugar then add bananas. Continue creaming the mixture, stopping to scrape down the batter from the sides of the bowl periodically.

3. Add eggs one at a time, scraping down the sides after each addition.

4. Combine buttermilk and baking soda and add to banana mixture on low speed.

5. Combine flour and bran.

6. Add the coffee alternately with the flour mixture, beating to combine.

7. Fold in the nuts.

8. Using an ice cream scoop, add one full scoop of batter to each paper cup. Bake at 400 degrees for 20 minutes.

Pumpkin Oat Nut Muffins

Because these muffins are so delicious, I doubled the batch so you will have plenty. They keep really well, and are great the second day, which you can't say about most baked goods. Slather on some walnut butter straight out of the oven and these will send you straight to heaven!

makes 12 muffins

Ingredients

2 cups puréed pumpkin
1 1/2 cups light or dark brown sugar, packed
1 cup vegetable oil
1/2 cup milk
2 eggs
2 teaspoons vanilla
2 1/2 cups old-fashioned oats
2 cups flour
1 cup walnuts, chopped
2 teaspoons baking powder
2 teaspoons cinnamon
1 teaspoon baking soda
1 teaspoon salt

1. Combine pumpkin, brown sugar, oil, milk, eggs, and vanilla in a mixer.

2. Add the remaining ingredients and beat thoroughly.

3. Refrigerate the batter for at least an hour before baking so that the oats have time to absorb the liquid. Batter will be somewhat thick. (Can be made the day before baking.)

3. Line a muffin tin with paper cups and spray each liner with nonstick spray. Using an ice cream scoop, add one full scoop to each paper cup. Bake in a preheated 350 degree.

Lemon Sun-Dried Cherry Scone

makes 12 scones

Ingredients

2 lemons and 2 oranges
2 sticks cold butter, cut into small cubes
4 cups flour
2 Tablespoons baking powder
1 Tablespoon sugar
1 teaspoon salt
1 cup sun-dried cherries
4 eggs
1/2 cup heavy cream
Sugar for topping

1. Zest the lemons and oranges and set aside.

2. Cut up your butter and keep chilled until ready to use.

3. In a large bowl, combine flour, baking powder, sugar and salt with the zests and cherries.

4. Using a pastry cutter, cut your butter into the dry ingredients until pea-sized.

5. In a separate bowl, whisk together the eggs and cream, reserving a tablespoon for the final glaze.

6. Make a well in the center, add the egg/cream mixture, and stir with a fork until just combined.

7. Turn dough out onto a floured board and knead a few times, taking care not to over knead.

8. Shape dough into a circle and roll out to 1 1/2 inches thick.

9. Cut crosswise into diamond shapes and place, at least 1-inch apart, on baking sheet sprayed with nonstick spray.

10. Chill for 10 to 15 minutes.

11. When ready to bake, brush the tops with the reserved egg mixture and sprinkle lightly with sugar. Bake at 400 degrees for 25 minutes or until golden brown.

Marionberry Pecan Streusel Coffeecake

serves 12

Ingredients

2 1/4 cups flour
1 cup brown sugar
3/4 cup sugar
3/4 cup oil
3 teaspoons cinnamon
1/2 teaspoon salt
1/4 teaspoon ground ginger
1 cup pecans, chopped
1 teaspoon baking soda
1 teaspoon baking powder
1 egg, beaten
1 cup buttermilk
1 cup fresh or frozen marionberries

1. In a large bowl, combine the flour, brown sugar, sugar, oil, 2 teaspoons of the cinnamon, salt and ginger.

2. Set aside 3/4 cup of this mixture for the topping, adding 1 more teaspoon cinnamon and the chopped pecans.

3. To the remaining batter add the baking soda, baking powder, egg and buttermilk.

4. Whisk to combine.

5. Dredge berries in a sprinkling of flour and fold into the batter. Do not over mix or the berries will color the batter.

6. Pour batter into a greased 9-inch-by-13-inch pan. Sprinkle the topping on the batter and bake at 350 degrees for 45 minutes. Insert the tip of a thin-bladed knife into the center of the cake to test that the batter is cooked all the way through. Best served warm.

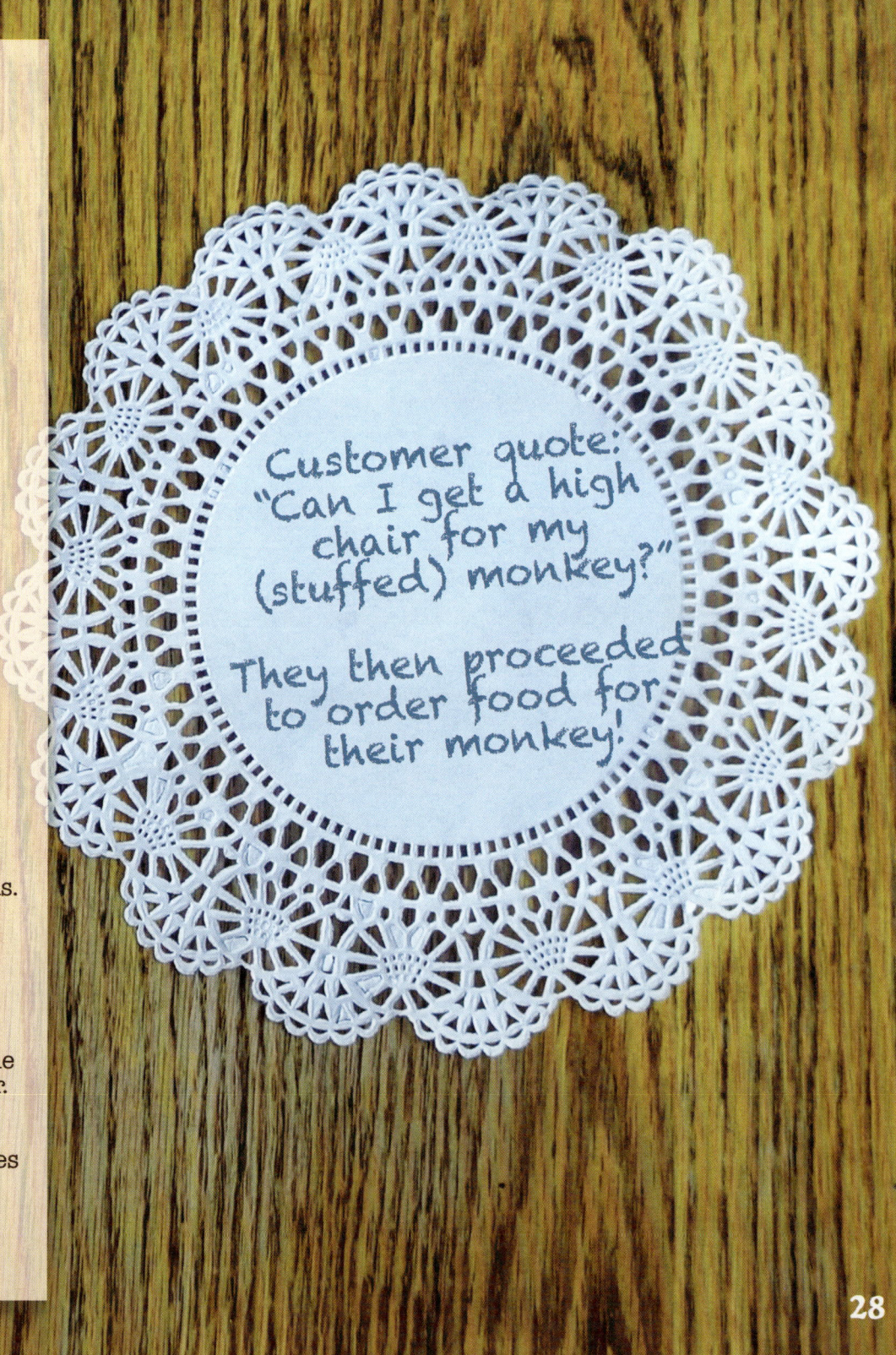

Customer quote: "Can I get a high chair for my (stuffed) monkey?"

They then proceeded to order food for their monkey!

Orange Cream Biscuit

These biscuits are wonderful! Split in half for the base for Eggs Benedict, or serve hot out of the oven with a generous slather of butter.

makes 12 biscuits

Ingredients

1 3/4 cups all-purpose flour
2 teaspoons sugar
2 teaspoons baking powder
1 teaspoon cream of tartar
1 teaspoon salt
1 Tablespoon orange zest
1 cup cold vegetable shortening
1 cup half and half

1. In a large bowl, combine the dry ingredients with the zest.

2. Using a pastry cutter, cut in the vegetable shortening until pea sized.

3. Make a well and add the half and half, stirring with a fork.

4. Turn out onto a floured board and knead 12- 15 times. Do not over knead.

5. Roll out to one inch thick and cut with a 2-to-3 inch biscuit cutter.

6. Place on a greased sheet pan, about 1-inch apart sand bake at 425 degrees for 20 minutes or until golden brown.

I arrived in Colorado in 1977, at the age of 17, the day after I graduated from high school. What was supposed to be just a summer job at Lane's Guest Ranch, until I went to college in the fall, became a decision that forever changed my life.

During the course of that summer, I realized that I wasn't ready to go to college that fall and Allenspark, Colorado became my new mountain home.

At 8500 feet, Allenspark is located at the base of Longs Peak in Rocky Mountain National Park. I fell in love with the tiny community of "old timers" and "long hairs", as they were affectionately known. A community that boasted a post office (where everyone gathered), a lodge, horse stables and two restaurants; one being The Meadow Mountain Cafe.

The Meadow Mountain Cafe (still in operation today!) is a small community cafe that had just opened and I went there after the ranch closed for the season, to seek employment. Winter was coming and I had to make ends meet. Dorothy Mueller was the chef/owner and we quickly hit it off. I started out waiting tables but eventually realized that I might be good at cooking.

Everything was made in-house, from our own bread, to our own yogurt and sprouts. Breakfast time was when everyone came to sit and gossip around our tiny wood stove in the dining room. I absolutely fell in love with the whole restaurant scene and the sense of community that it brought. I started cooking and never looked back.

My very first cabin in the woods. I paid $75.00 a month for rent and it had no electricity or running water. There was a spring nearby from where I hauled water up a hill (I had no car) and somehow I gathered firewood for the old wood cookstove.

Age: 19 Year: 1979

By the time I was twenty four, I knew that it was time to take the next major step and apply to cooking school. It was time to leave my beloved mountain town and so I called my parents to let them know and they were thrilled. Their hippy mountain child was finally getting serious about her career and I wanted my own restaurant.

Patty #1   Allison   Dorothy   Johnny   Patty #2

The Meadow Mountain Crew

Thank you Dorothy Mueller-Christine for your support and inspiration!

Hello, Morning Glory?

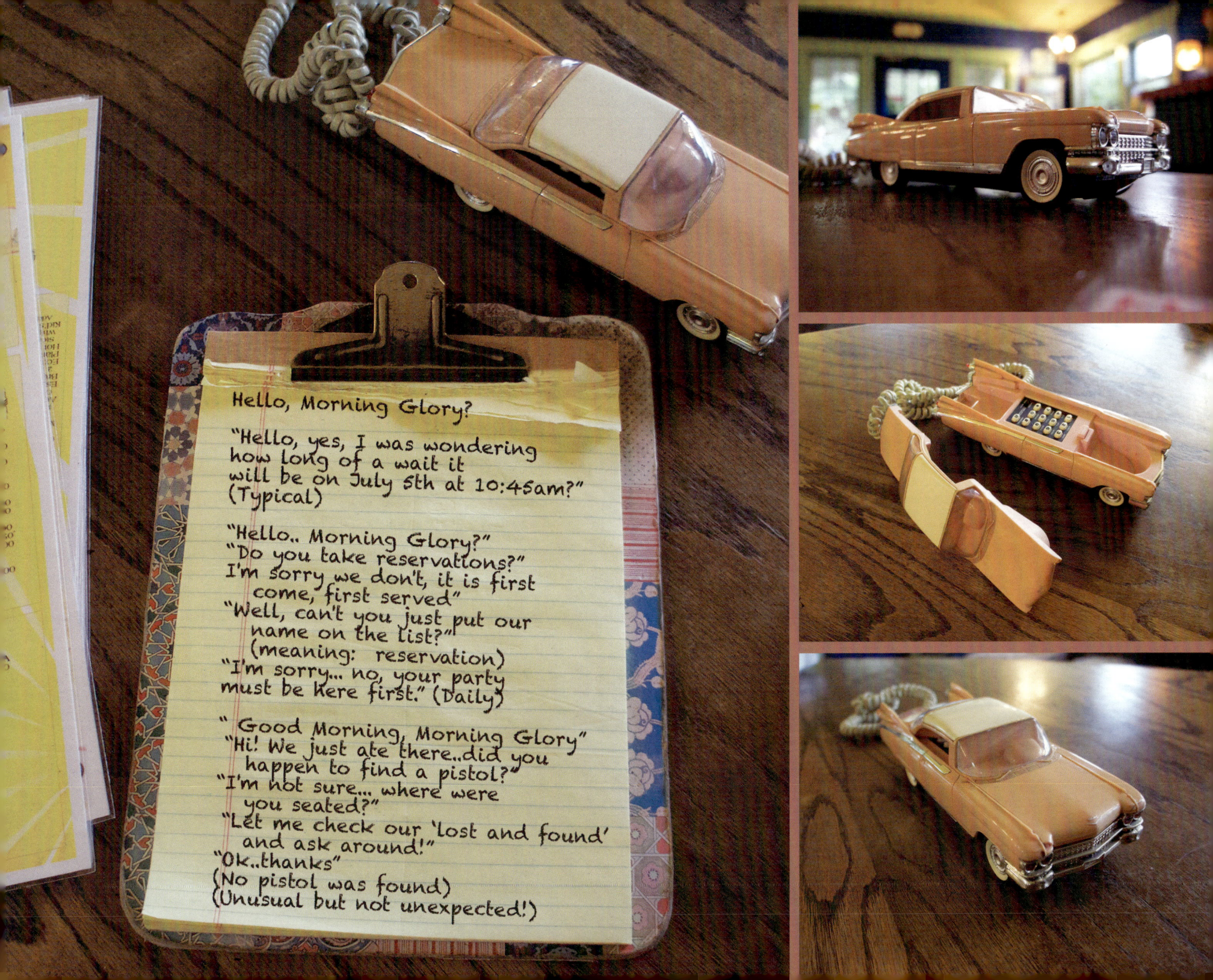

"Hello, yes, I was wondering how long of a wait it will be on July 5th at 10:45am?" (Typical)

"Hello.. Morning Glory?"
"Do you take reservations?"
"I'm sorry we don't, it is first come, first served"
"Well, can't you just put our name on the list?"
(meaning: reservation)
"I'm sorry... no, your party must be here first." (Daily)

"Good Morning, Morning Glory"
"Hi! We just ate there..did you happen to find a pistol?"
"I'm not sure... where were you seated?"
"Let me check our 'lost and found' and ask around!"
"Ok..thanks"
(No pistol was found)
(Unusual but not unexpected!)

Cakes, Waffles & French Toast

Cakes, Waffles and French Toast

Cakes

Oatmeal Pancakes with Walnut Butter 38
Buckwheat Banana Pancakes 40
Orange Blueberry Pancakes with Walnut Butter 42
Sour Cream Marionberry Pancakes 44
White Chocolate Pancakes with Lemon Butter and Fresh Raspberries 46
Pumpkin Oat Pancakes 48

Waffles

Lemon Poppyseed Waffles 50
Buttermilk Waffle or Pancakes 52
Gingerbread Waffle with Apple Compote and Whipped Cream 54
Whole Grain Pecan Waffles 56
Coconut Almond Waffles 58

French Toast

French Toast 101 60
Marionberry Stuffed French Toast with Lemon Butter, Marionberry
  Syrup and Toasted Almonds 62
Nutella Stuffed French Toast with Amaretto Hazelnut Butter and
  Dark Cherry Syrup 64
Lemon Ricotta French Toast with Lemon Butter and Raspberry Syrup 66
Coconut Cheesecake Stuffed French Toast with Lemon Butter, Mango
  Syrup and Macadamia Nuts 68
Cheese Blintzes with Whipped Cream and Marionberry Syrup 70

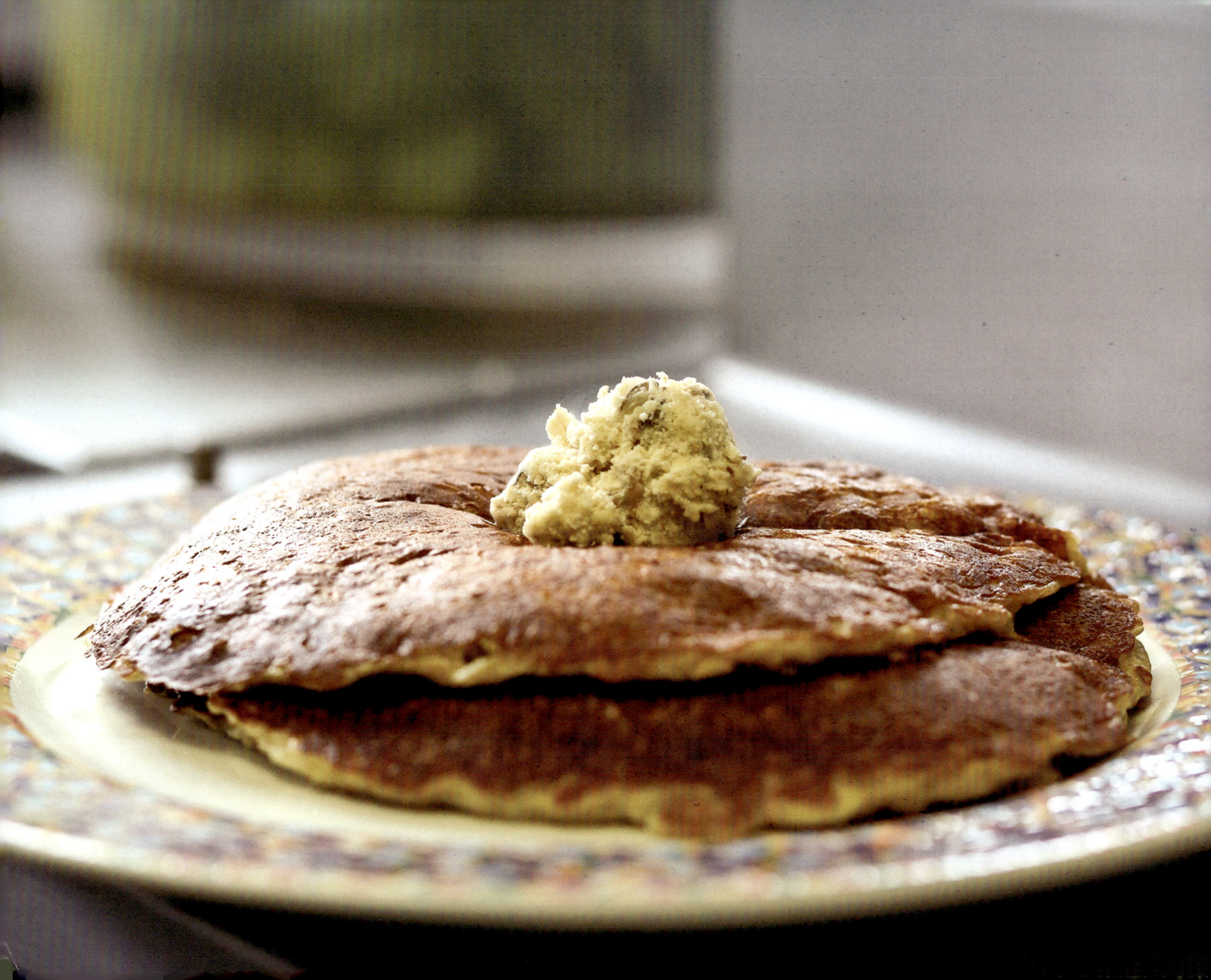

Oatmeal Pancakes

These pancakes are a huge favorite at Morning Glory and this is our most requested recipe.
They have great oatmeal flavor and will keep you going all day long.
The batter is best made the day before serving so that the oats have time to absorb the buttermilk.
Serve with walnut butter (see recipe in Finishing Touches) and your favorite syrup.

serves 2 to 4

Ingredients

2 cups old fashioned oats
2 1/4 cups buttermilk
1/4 cup vegetable oil
2 eggs, beaten
1/2 cup flour
1/4 cup brown sugar
1/8 cup white sugar
1 1/2 teaspoons baking powder
1 teaspoon baking soda
1 teaspoon salt

1. Combine the oats, buttermilk, oil and eggs in a large bowl.

2. Sift together the remaining ingredients and add to oat mixture. Mix to combine. Cover and store in refrigerator. You may need to adjust batter by adding a bit more buttermilk before cooking.

3. Spoon batter onto a pre-heated, greased griddle.

4. Flip over when golden brown on the bottom, and continue cooking until firm to the touch—about 5 to 7 minutes.

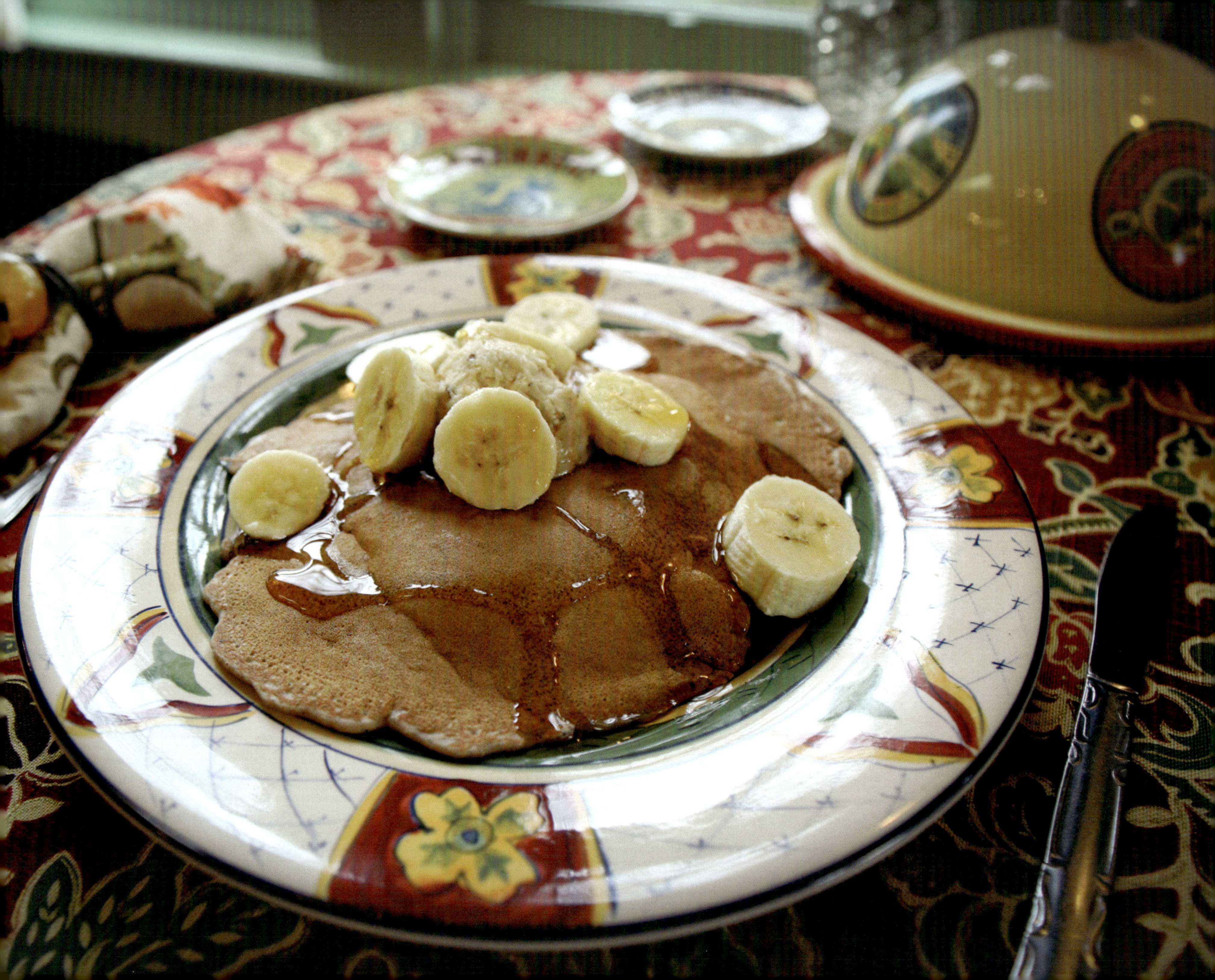

Buckwheat Banana Pancakes

These wonderfully thin pancakes have a richness to them that comes from the addition of cocoa. The batter seems thin but thickens as it rests. Best if made the day before serving, covered and refrigerated. Just slice your bananas and add to the batter or serve on top. We do both.
Serve with walnut butter or lemon butter (see recipes in the Finishing Touches section) and pure maple syrup.

serves 2 to 4

Ingredients

2 cups flour
1 cup buckwheat flour
1/2 cup sugar
6 Tablespoons cocoa powder
4 teaspoons baking powder
1 teaspoon salt
4 eggs
4 cups milk
1/2 cup vegetable oil

1. Combine flour, buckwheat, cocoa, sugar, baking powder and salt in large bowl.

2. Whisk together eggs, milk and vegetable oil and add to the dry mix; whisk to combine.

3. Cook on a hot, greased pancake griddle.

4. Flip when bubbles appear on the tops and cook for 2 more minutes.

Customer quote:
"We are energetically sensitive, and the spirits from the 'Third chakra' told us that we are going to need a booth."

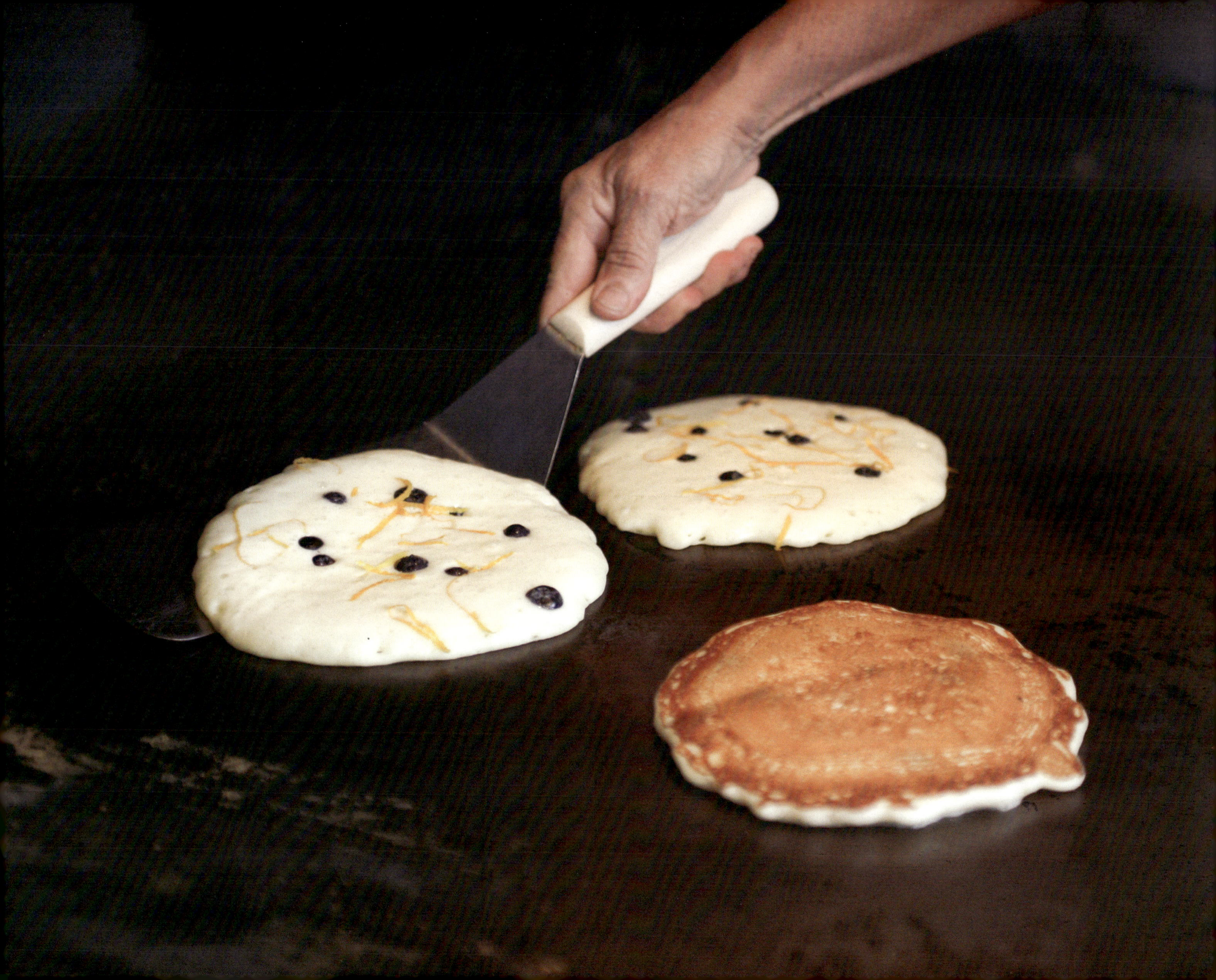

Orange Blueberry Pancakes

serves 2 to 4
Ingredients

4 1/2 cups buttermilk
5 eggs
1/4 cup orange juice
1 Tablespoon orange extract
4 1/2 cups flour
1/2 cup sugar
2 teaspoons baking soda
2 teaspoons salt
3 sticks butter, melted
Zest of one orange
1 cup fresh or frozen blueberries

1. Whisk together buttermilk, eggs, orange juice and orange extract in a medium bowl.

2. In separate bowl, sift together flour, sugar, baking soda, and salt.

3. Add wet ingredients to dry ingredients, stir in butter and zest and whisk to combine.

4. Spoon the batter onto a pre-heated griddle and sprinkle berries onto each pancake.

5. Flip when bubbles start to appear and the pancakes are golden on the bottom.

6. Cook for a few more minutes.

To serve, top with Walnut Butter or Lemon Butter (see recipes in The Finishing Touches section). Delicious with pure maple or blueberry syrup.

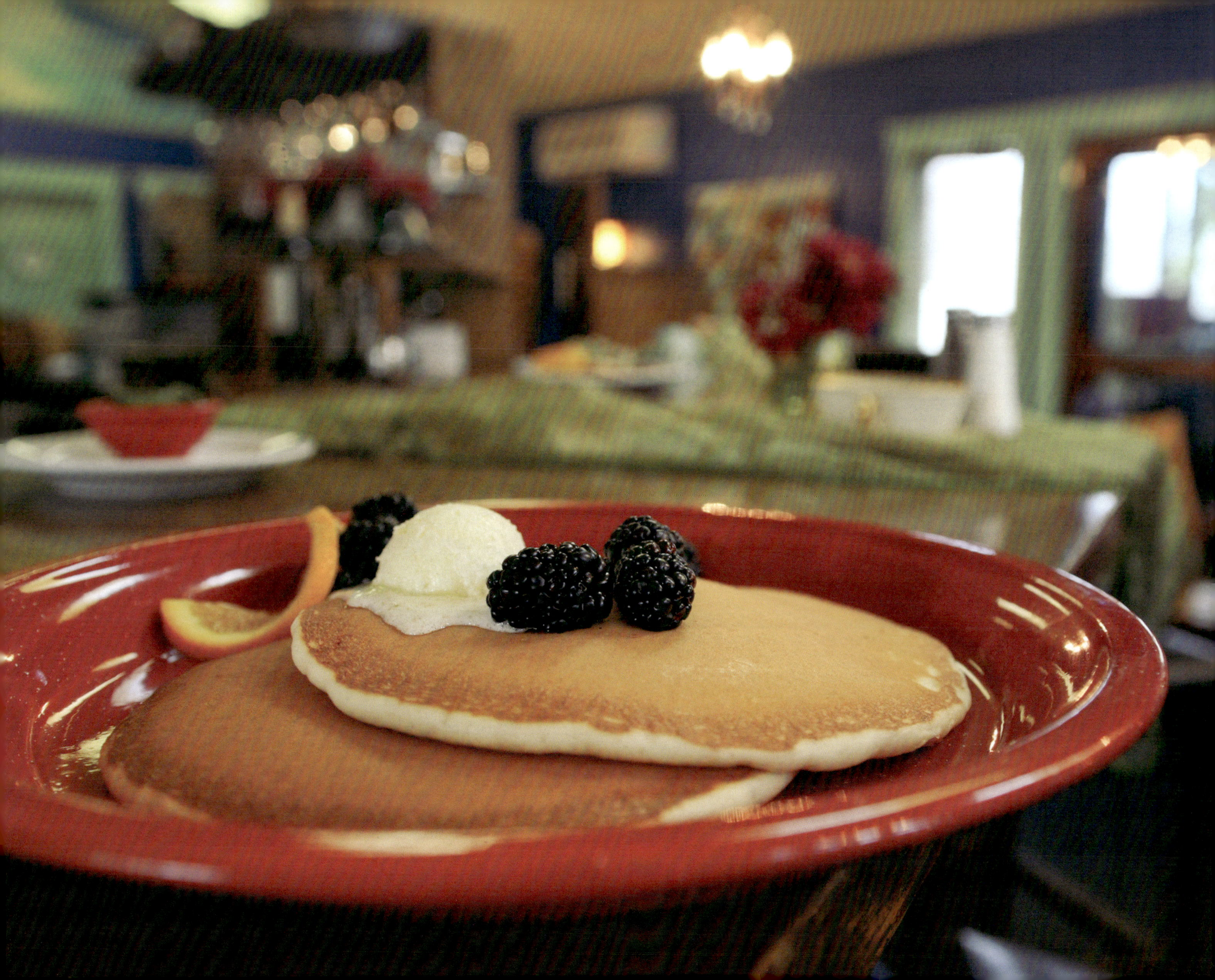

Sour Cream Marionberry Pancakes

serves 2 to 4

Ingredients

2 eggs
1 cup sour cream
1 cup milk
2 cups flour
1/2 cup sugar
1 teaspoon salt
1 teaspoon baking powder
1 stick butter, melted
1 teaspoon lemon zest, chopped
1 cup fresh marionberries

1. Combine eggs, sour cream, and milk. Sift together flour, sugar, salt and baking powder in a mixing bowl.

2. Combine wet ingredients with dry ingredients, melted butter and lemon zest.

3. Whisk to combine, but do not over mix.

4. Ladle batter on a hot, pre-heated, greased griddle, flipping when bubbles appear and bottoms are golden brown. Top with Lemon Butter (recipe in Finishing Touches section) and fresh Marionberries.

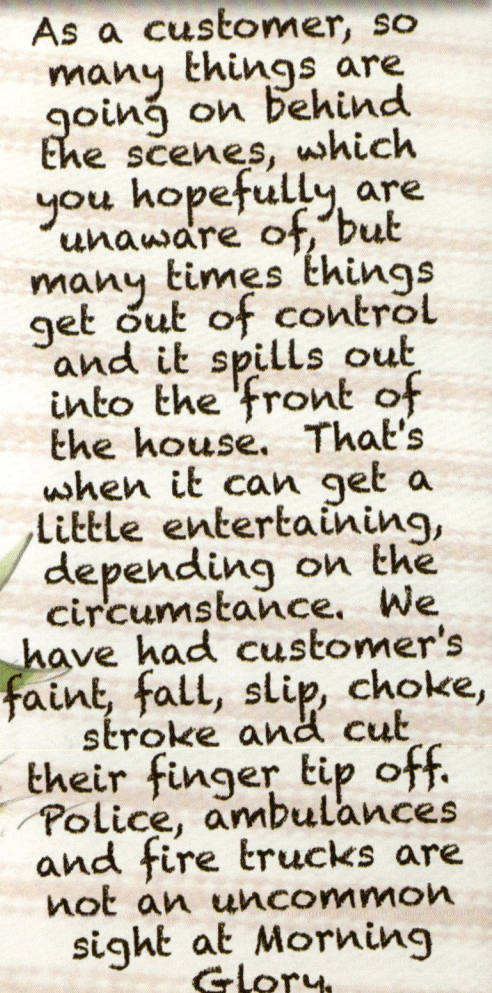

As a customer, so many things are going on behind the scenes, which you hopefully are unaware of, but many times things get out of control and it spills out into the front of the house. That's when it can get a little entertaining, depending on the circumstance. We have had customer's faint, fall, slip, choke, stroke and cut their finger tip off. Police, ambulances and fire trucks are not an uncommon sight at Morning Glory.

44

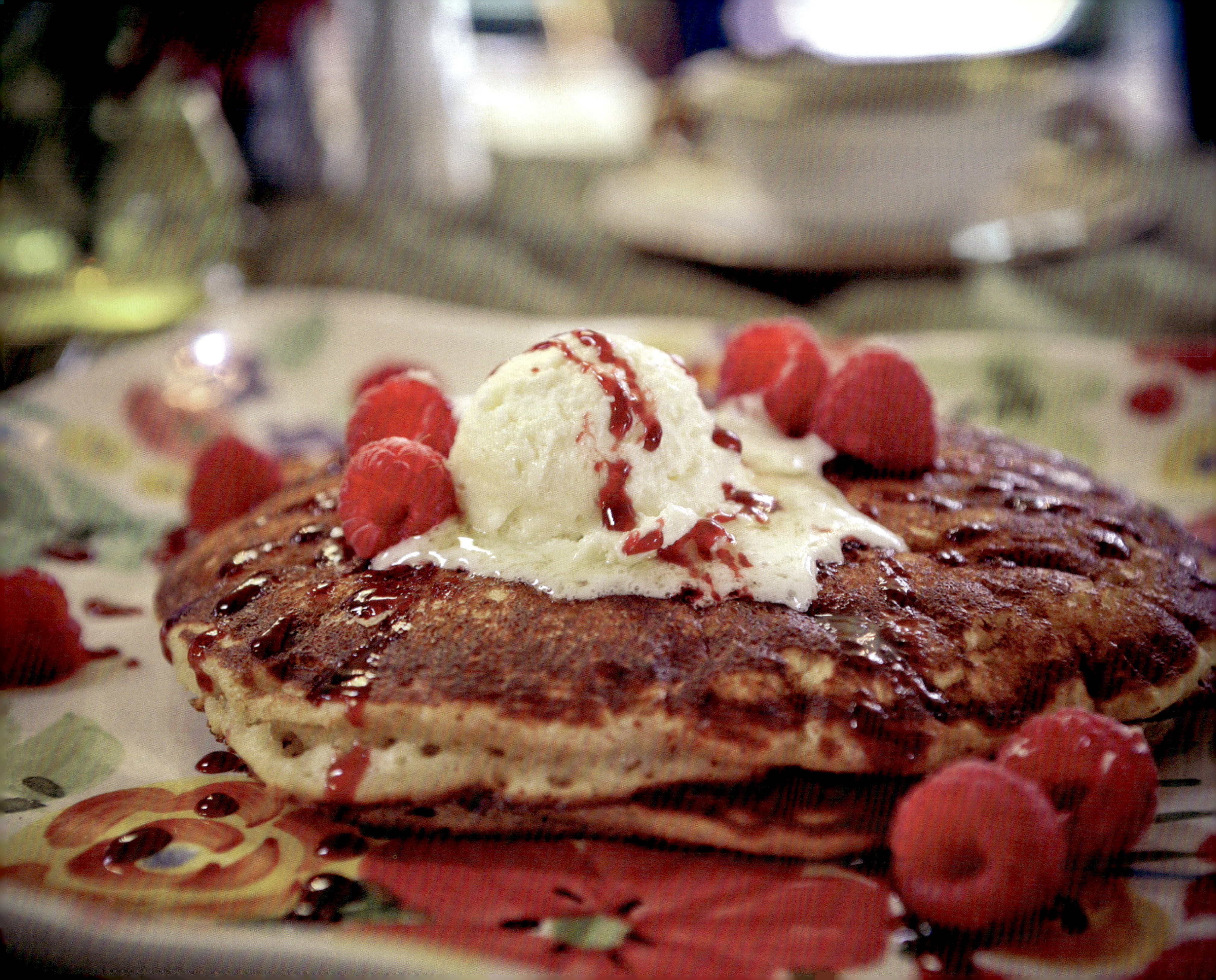

White Chocolate Raspberry Pancakes with Lemon Butter, Raspberry Syrup and Fresh Raspberries

serves 2 to 4

Ingredients

1 stick butter
1 Tablespoon lemon juice
2 eggs
1 cup buttermilk
2 cups flour
1/2 cup Ghirardelli white chocolate powder
1 Tablespoon baking soda
1 teaspoon salt
2 cups fresh raspberries, divided
1/2 cup sugar

1. Melt lemon juice and butter together.

2. Whisk together eggs and buttermilk.

3. In a mixing bowl, sift together flour, white chocolate powder, baking soda and salt.

4. Mix in buttermilk mixture and lemon/butter mixture until well-combined.

5. Cook on a hot, greased pancake griddle.

6. Flip when bubbles appear on the tops and cook for 2 more minutes.

Top with Lemon Butter, Raspberry Syrup (See recipes in Finishing Touches) and fresh raspberries.

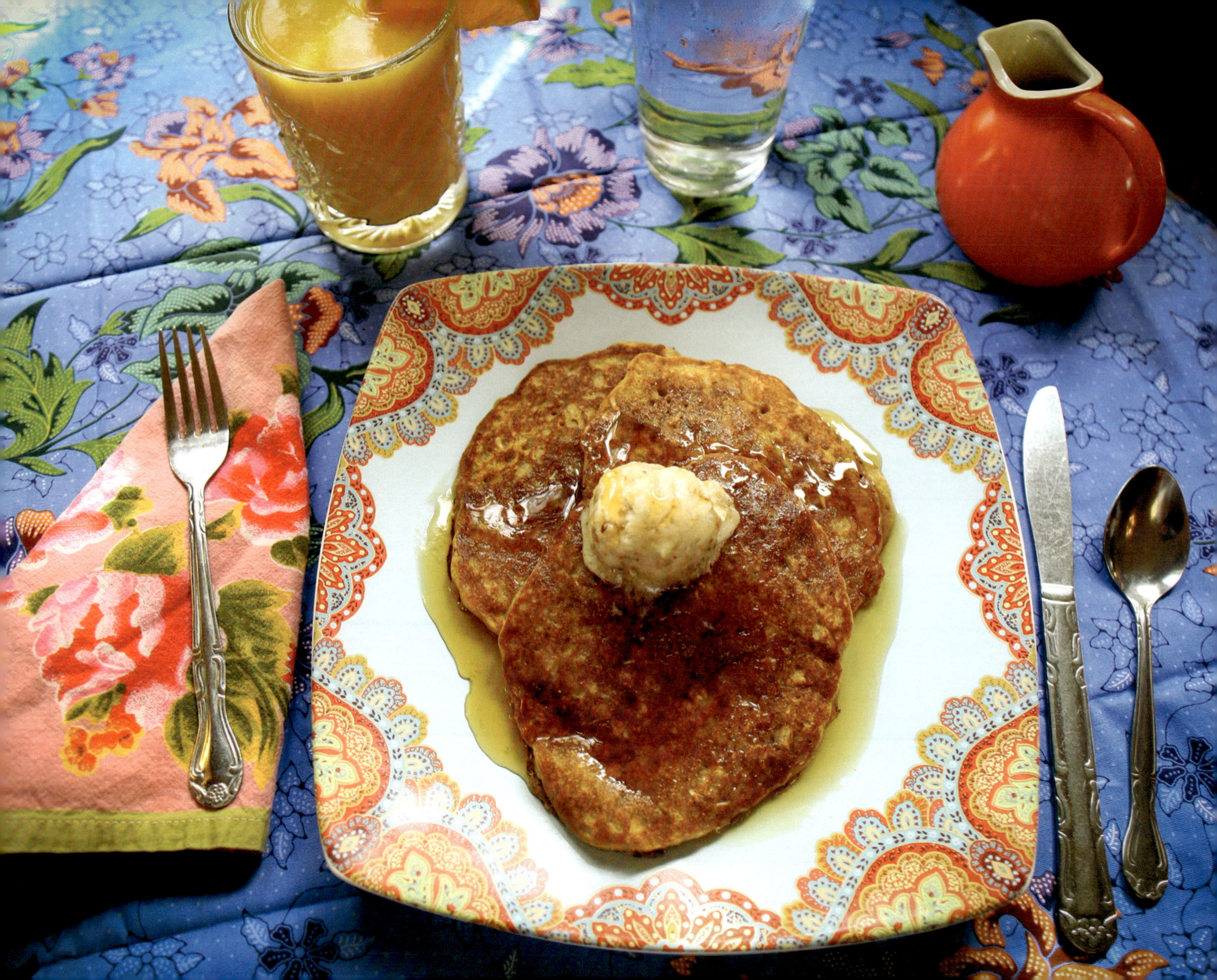

Pumpkin Oat Pancakes

Great for the holidays.

serves 2 to 4

~ Ingredients ~

1/4 cup pumpkin purée
2 eggs
2 cups buttermilk
2 cups flour
1 cup whole oats
1/4 cup brown sugar
1/8 cup sugar
2 teaspoons baking powder
2 teaspoons baking soda
1 teaspoon salt
1 teaspoon ground ginger
1 teaspoon ground cinnamon
1/2 teaspoon ground cloves
2 sticks butter, melted

1. Whisk together pumpkin purée and eggs in a large mixing bowl; add buttermilk.

2. Add remaining ingredients except for the melted butter, mix thoroughly, then slowly fold in butter.

3. Cook pancakes on a medium-hot, pre-heated greased griddle, flipping when bubbles appear and pancakes are golden brown. (You may need to adjust the thickness of the batter if it sits overnight because the oats will absorb a lot of the moisture, so add a little more buttermilk as needed.)

Serve with Walnut Butter and your favorite syrup.

Lost and Found

What customer's have left behind: socks, shoes, underwear, (there was once a pair of granny panties floating around the lobby) books, hats, wedding rings, stroller's, bicycles. You name it, it has been left here.

Stolen items:
Tables, chairs, safes, equipment, bicycles, planter boxes, tapestries, art work and anything that hasn't been nailed down.

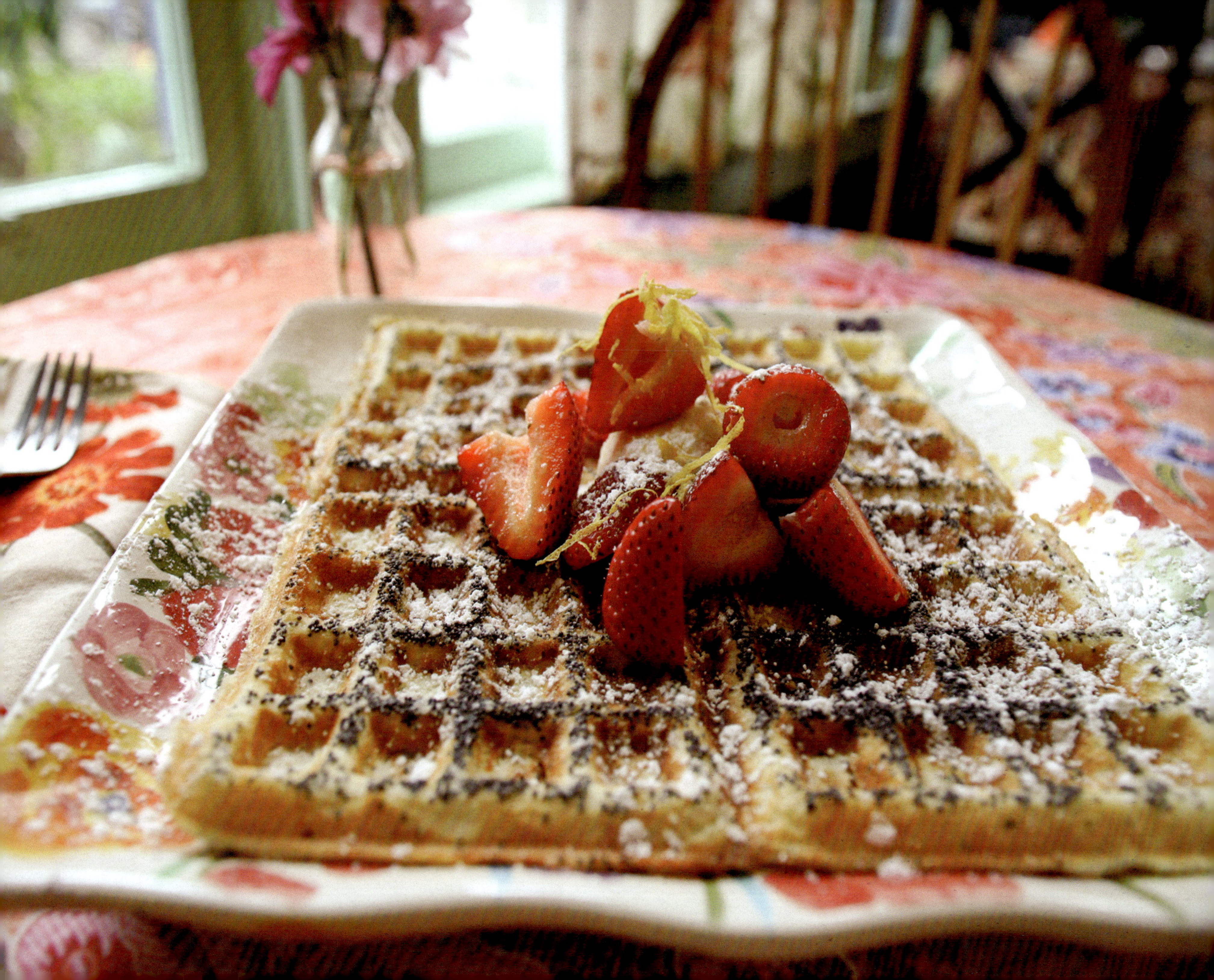

Lemon Poppyseed Waffles

We use domestic waffle irons at the restaurant. I prefer large Belgian-style makers with four squares instead of the standard two. Before making your batter, be sure to preheat your iron.

serves 4 to 6

Ingredients

5 eggs
4 1/2 cups buttermilk
1/4 cup lemon juice
1 Tablespoon lemon extract
4 1/2 cups flour
1/2 cup sugar
1/4 cup poppy seeds
2 teaspoons salt
2 teaspoons baking soda
3 sticks butter, melted
Zest of 2 lemons, chopped
Powdered sugar
Fresh berries for serving

1. Preheat your waffle iron.

2. Whisk together eggs, buttermilk, lemon juice and lemon extract in a mixing bowl.

3. In a separate large bowl, sift together flour, sugar, poppy seeds, salt, and baking soda.

4. Add wet ingredients to dry ingredients and mix gently. Stir in melted butter and lemon zest, mixing just to combine.

5. Spray iron with non-stick spray, ladle batter into iron and spread evenly to edges. Close the lid and cook until golden brown.

Serve with Lemon Butter (see recipe in The Finishing Touches section), a sprinkling of powdered sugar and fresh berries.

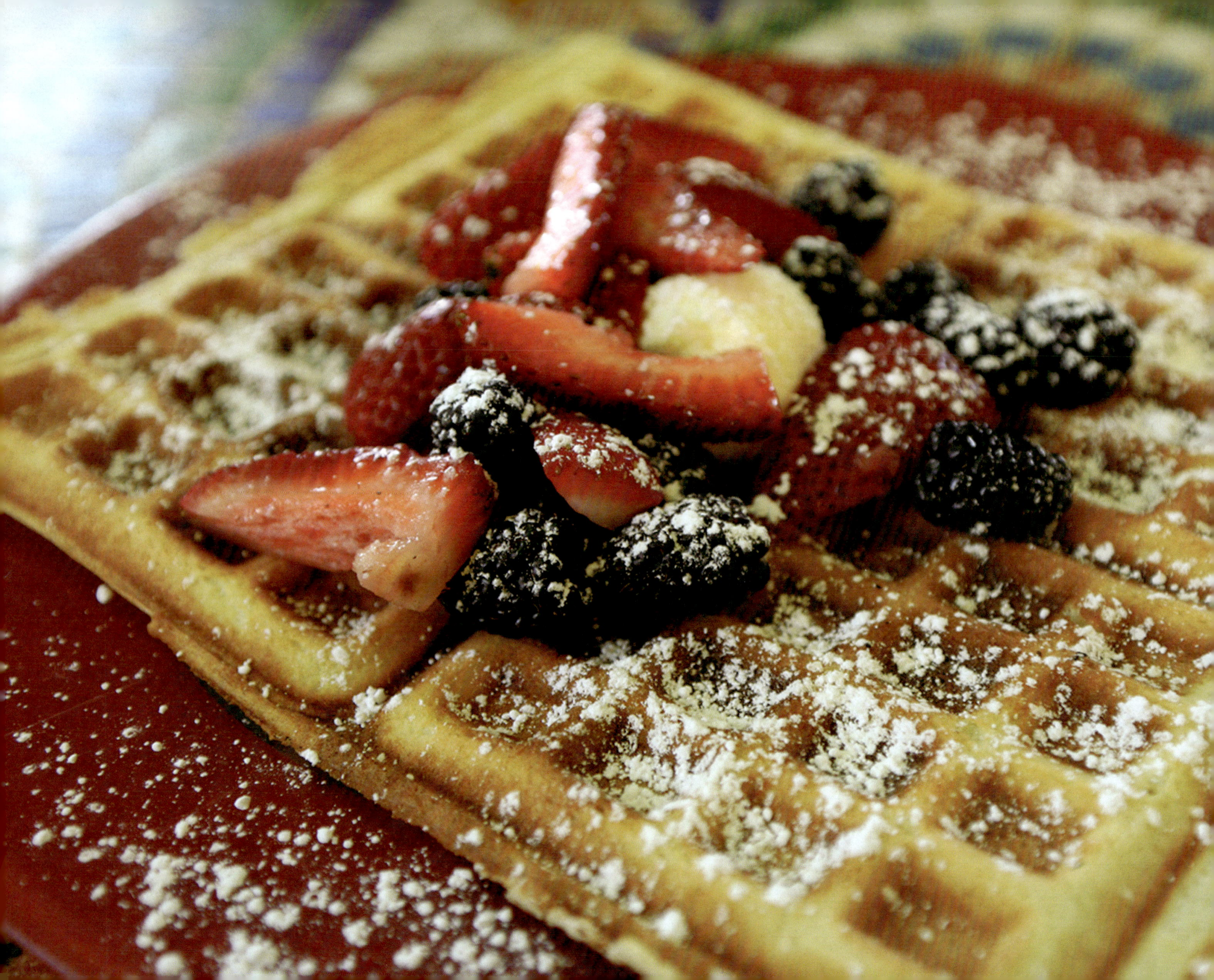

Buttermilk Waffles or Pancakes

We serve these with Lemon Butter and our homemade Marionberry syrup (see recipes in The Finishing Touches section) or pure maple syrup. The waffles are moist and crispy, or as pancakes, they are incredibly light and fluffy.

serves 2 to 4

Ingredients

2 cups buttermilk
1/4 cup vegetable oil
4 eggs
2 cups flour
1/2 cup sugar
1 Tablespoon baking powder
2 teaspoons salt

1. Whisk together the buttermilk, oil, and eggs.

2. In a mixing bowl, sift together the flour, sugar, baking powder, and salt.

3. Add to the dry ingredients and whisk to combine. Do not overmix.

4. Cook on preheated griddle or heated waffle iron until golden brown.

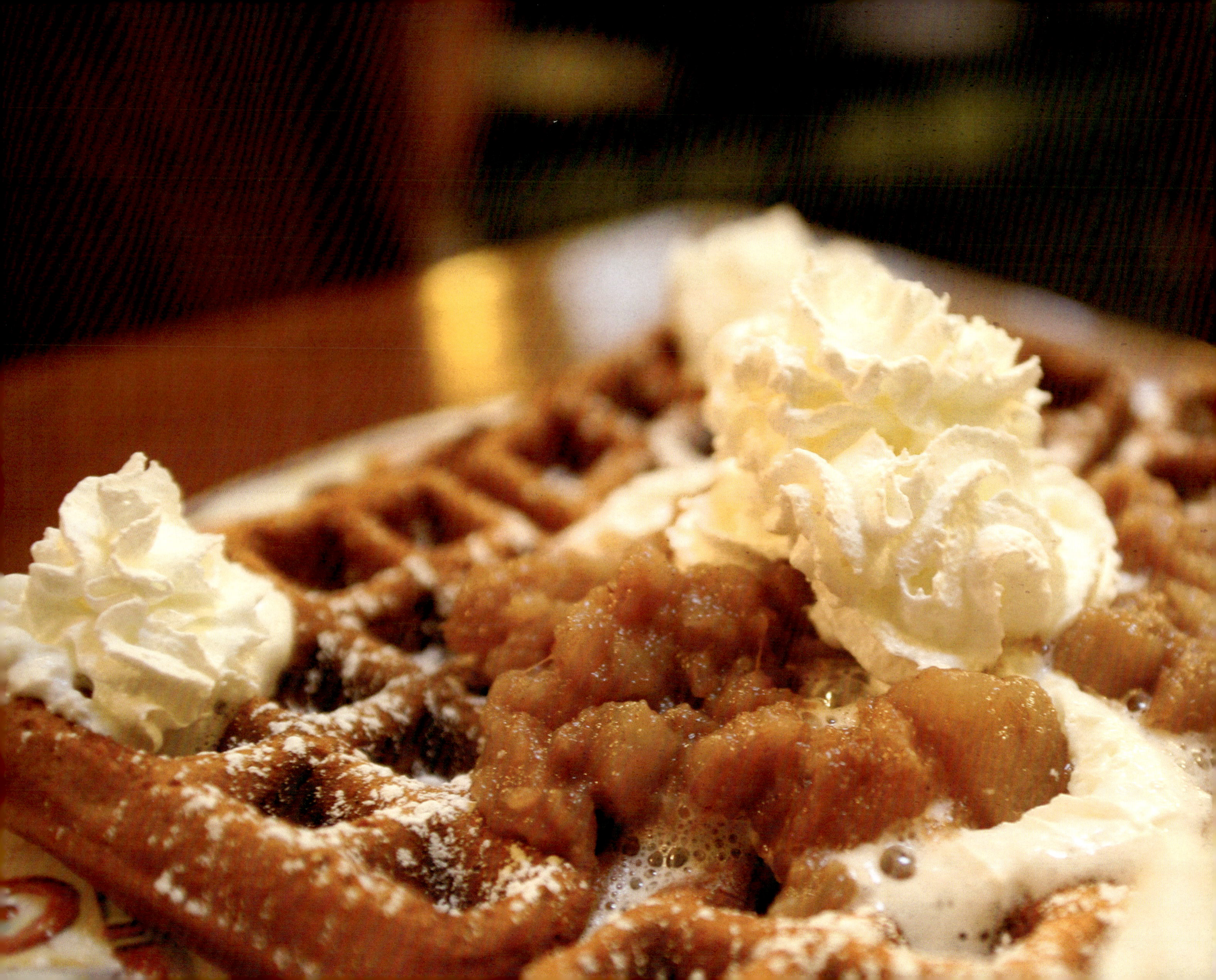

Gingerbread Waffles with Apple Compote and Whipped Cream

These are great during the fall or for a holiday brunch. The smell is intoxicating while they are cooking, and of course while you are devouring them.
If short on time just serve with fresh whipped cream and a dusting of powdered sugar.
(The Apple Compote really gives them that extra special flavor, though.)

serves 4 to 6

Ingredients

4 cups flour
1 Tablespoon baking powder
2 teaspoons ground cinnamon
2 teaspoons ground ginger
1 teaspoon ground cloves
2 teaspoons salt
2 1/4 cups milk
3/4 cup molasses
4 eggs
1/4 cup vegetable oil
2 cups heavy whipping cream, chilled
1/4 cup sugar
Powdered sugar

1. Combine flour, baking powder, cinnamon, ginger, cloves and salt in a large bowl.

2. In a separate bowl, whisk together the milk, molasses, eggs and oil; add to dry ingredients and whisk to combine.

3. Cook in preheated waffle iron sprayed with non-stick spray until golden brown.

4. Whip the cream and sugar together to desired thickness.

Top waffle with whipped cream, Apple Compote (see The Finishing Touches section) and a sprinkling of powdered sugar.

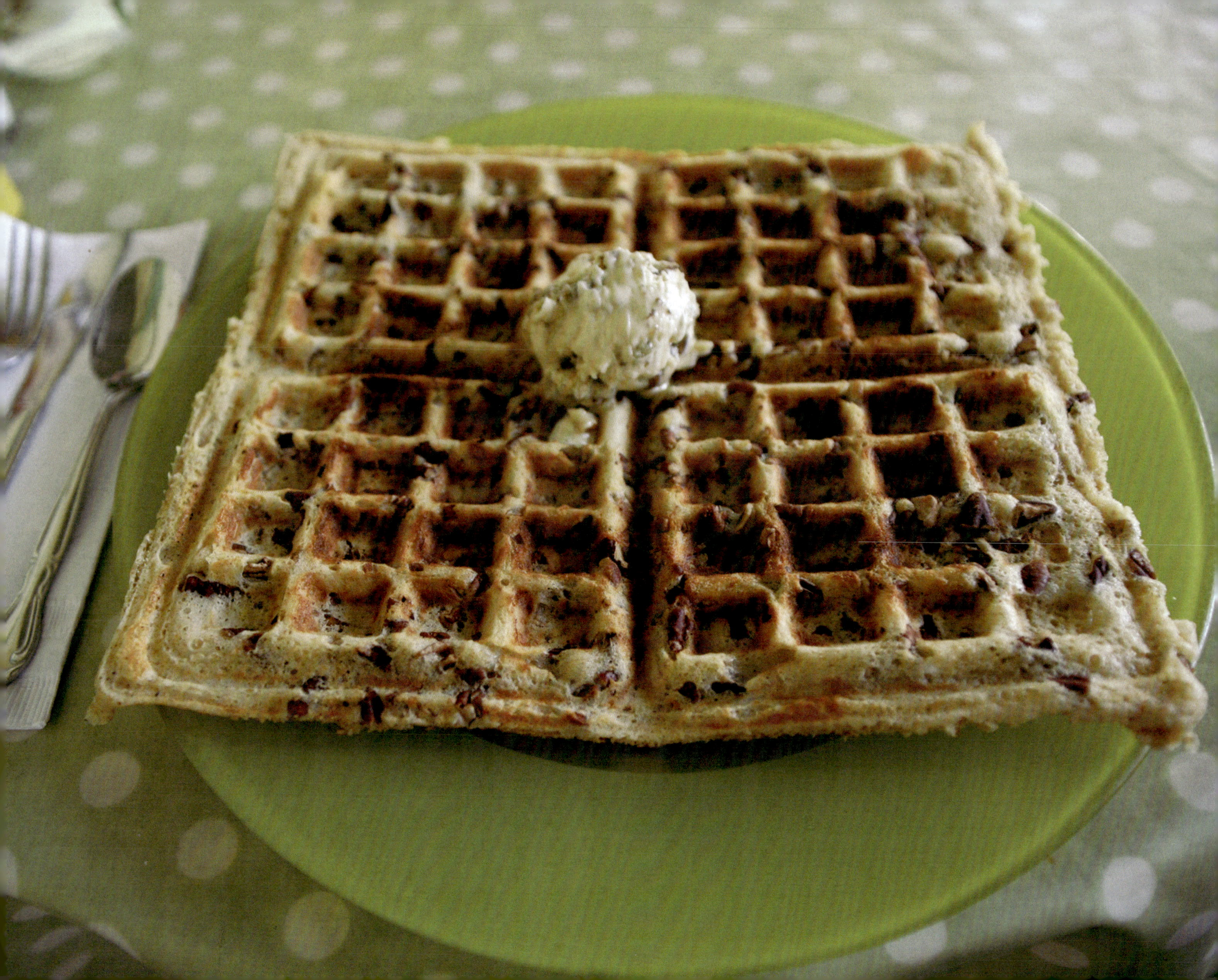

Whole Grain Pecan Waffle

This batter is great for waffles or pancakes—
just sprinkle the nuts on the bottom of the
pre-heated waffle iron before adding the batter,
or add nuts to the pancake before flipping
Delicious with Walnut Butter and pure maple syrup.

serves 2 to 4

Ingredients

2 cups buttermilk
4 large eggs
1/4 cup vegetable oil
2 Tablespoons brown sugar
1/2 cup graham flour
1/4 cup whole wheat flour
1 1/4 cups all-purpose flour
1/8 cup sugar
1 Tablespoon baking powder
1 teaspoon salt
1 cup toasted pecans

1. In a large mixing bowl, whisk together the buttermilk, eggs, oil and brown sugar.

2. In a separate bowl, stir together three flours, sugar, baking powder and salt; add to the liquid ingredients and whisk to combine.

3. For pancakes, cook on a pre-heated griddle, sprinkling pecans over the surface. For waffles, sprinkle pecans in preheated iron sprayed with non-stick spray.

4. Pour in batter, spread to the edges, and cook until golden brown.

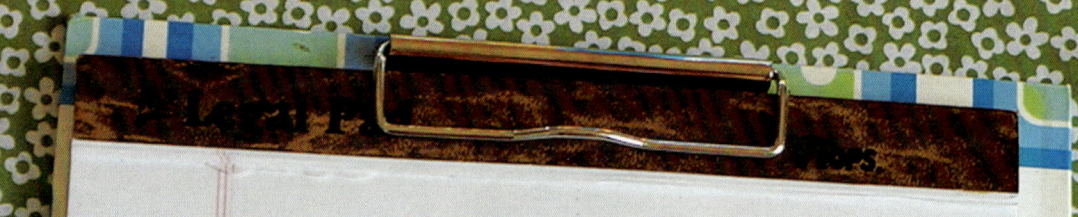

A typical day...

A man jumped out of the men's bathroom window, which was quite a drop, in order to evade his $13.00 bill. Dining and dashing happens more than you would think.

One day a woman dropped her wedding ring down the heating vent, and paid a waiter (Josh) to fetch it.

Someone once smashed open our french glass door to steal a six pack of beer.

Unbelieveably, someone broke into our basement (probably an employee) and wheeled away our safe, which I had yet to bolt to the floor. It was extremely heavy, so I have no idea how they got it out of there. The police later found it in an empty field, contents, un-opened.

Recently, a giant limb snapped off of our sweet gum tree out front, smashing our arbor and almost hitting two people. Thank goodness they heard the crack and were able to get out of the way!

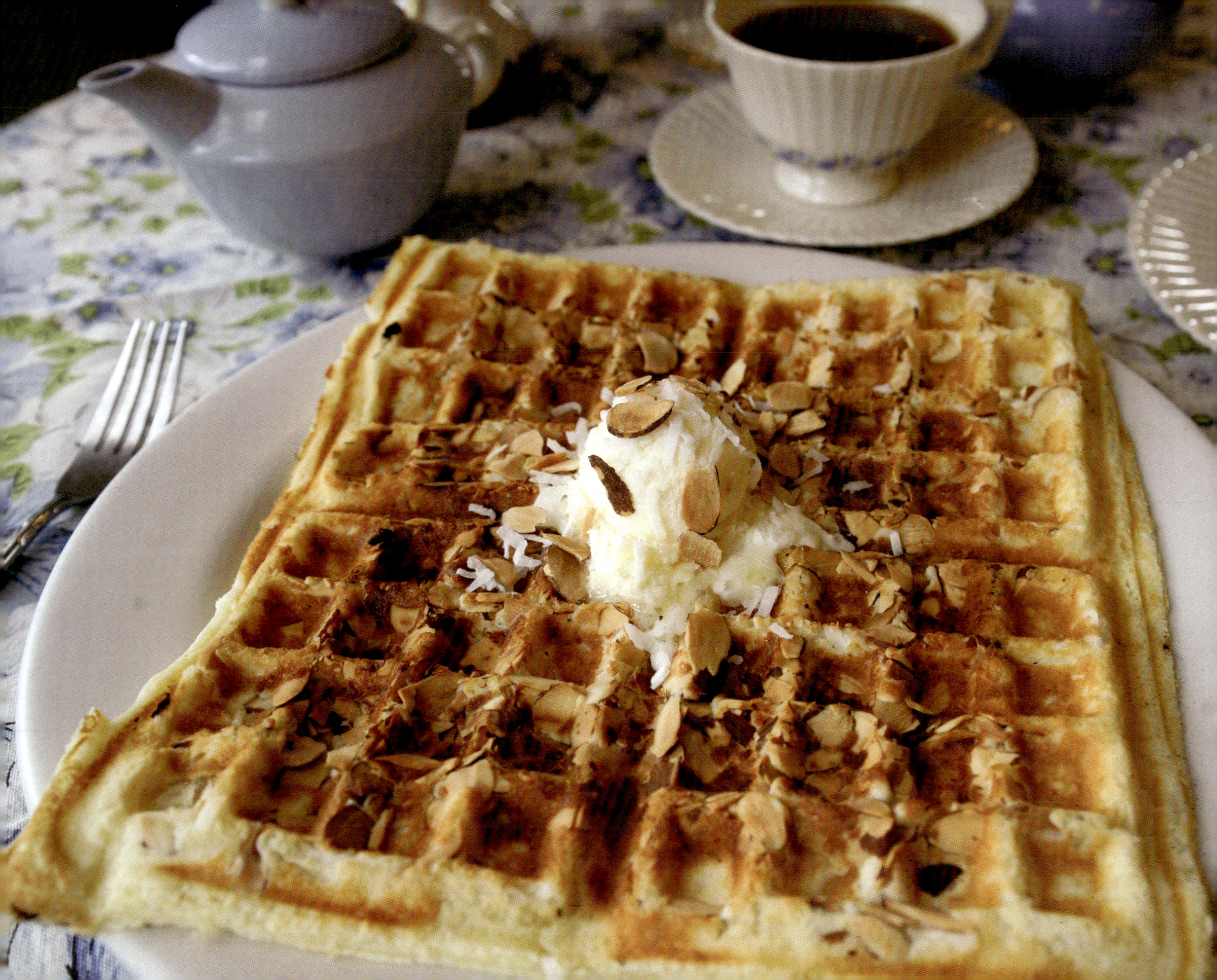

Coconut Almond Waffle

These waffles are moist and crispy, and the pancakes are incredibly light and fluffy. We serve them with Lemon Butter and our homemade Marionberry Syrup (see The Finishing Touches section) or pure maple syrup.

serves 2 to 4

Ingredients

2 cups buttermilk
4 eggs
1/4 cup vegetable oil
2 cups flour
1/2 cup sugar
1 Tablespoon baking powder
2 teaspoons salt
1 cup coconut, shredded
1 cup toasted almonds

1. In a mixing bowl, combine the buttermilk, eggs and oil.

2. Sift together the flour, sugar, baking powder and salt; add to wet ingredients and whisk to combine. Do not over mix.

3. Spread batter in pre-heated iron sprayed with non-stick spray, sprinkling coconut and almonds evenly over the batter.

4. Cook until golden brown.

Thoughts...

Morning Glory has now been open for 21 years and it is hard to describe what that feels like. I never got married, but owning a restaurant, is like being in a marriage, because sometimes you want a divorce! You wake up the next day though and realize what you have created and how much you are loved and you "Carry on". Ashland has embraced Morning Glory, as it's own and I love serving this community.

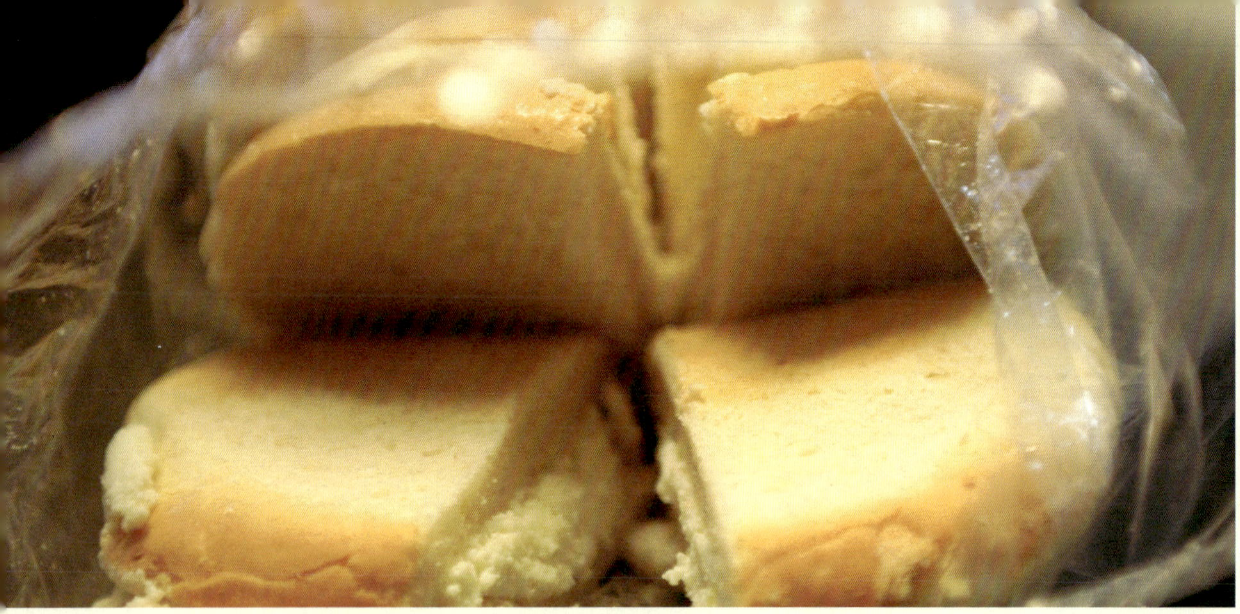
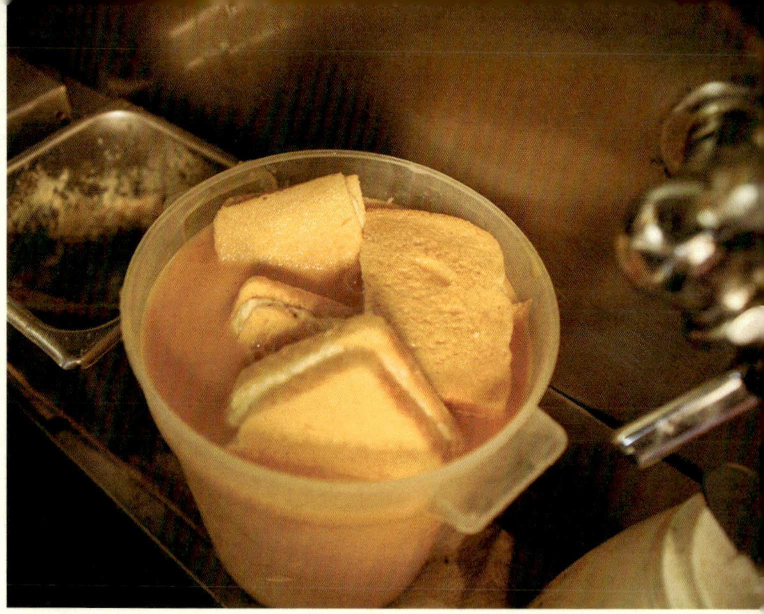
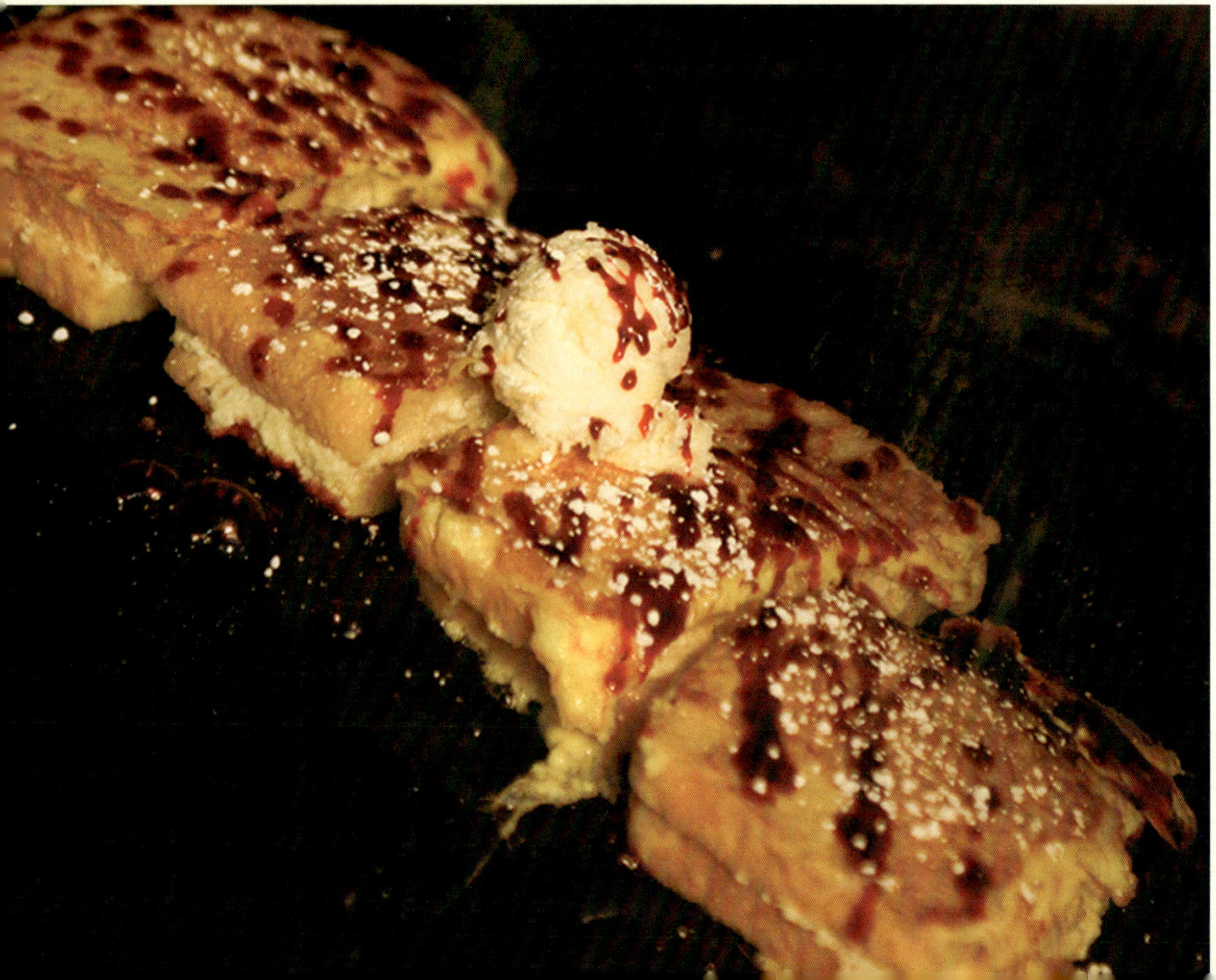
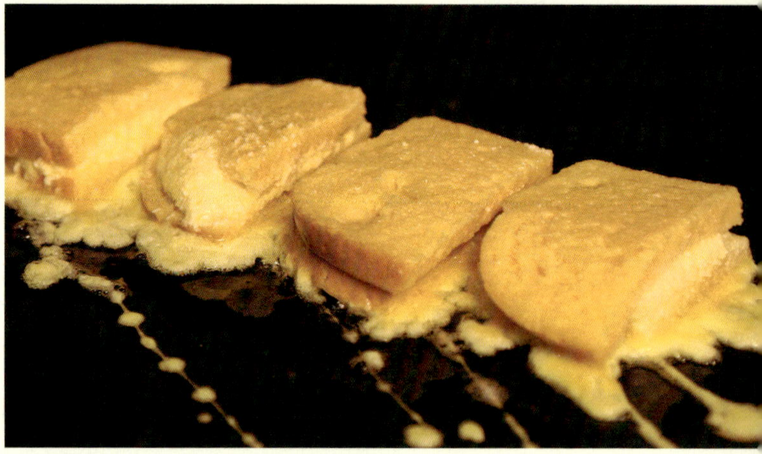
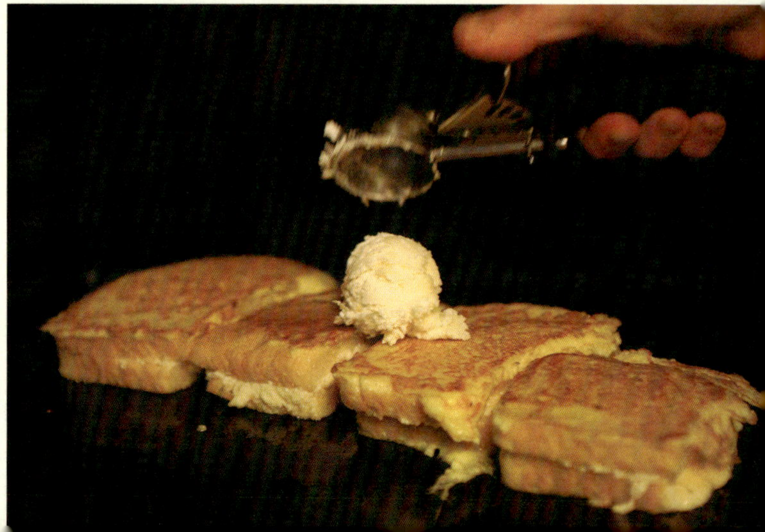

French Toast 101

Serves 6 to 8

Ingredients

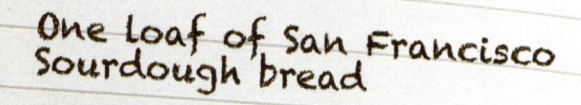

One loaf of San Francisco Sourdough bread

Batter:
6 eggs, whisked to combine
2 cups half and half
1/2 cup sugar
1 teaspoon vanilla

Butter and oil for cooking

To make the French toast:
1. Whisk batter ingredients together in a dish large enough to dip the bread.
2. On a heated flat griddle, melt some butter with some vegetable oil.

3. When the butter starts to foam, dip the bread in the batter, making sure that the whole piece is covered, and place on griddle.

4. When golden brown on bottom, turn over to cook the other side.

If you are cooking this in batches, place French Toast in a preheated oven to hold while other pieces cook. Before serving, add toppings as listed in the following recipes.

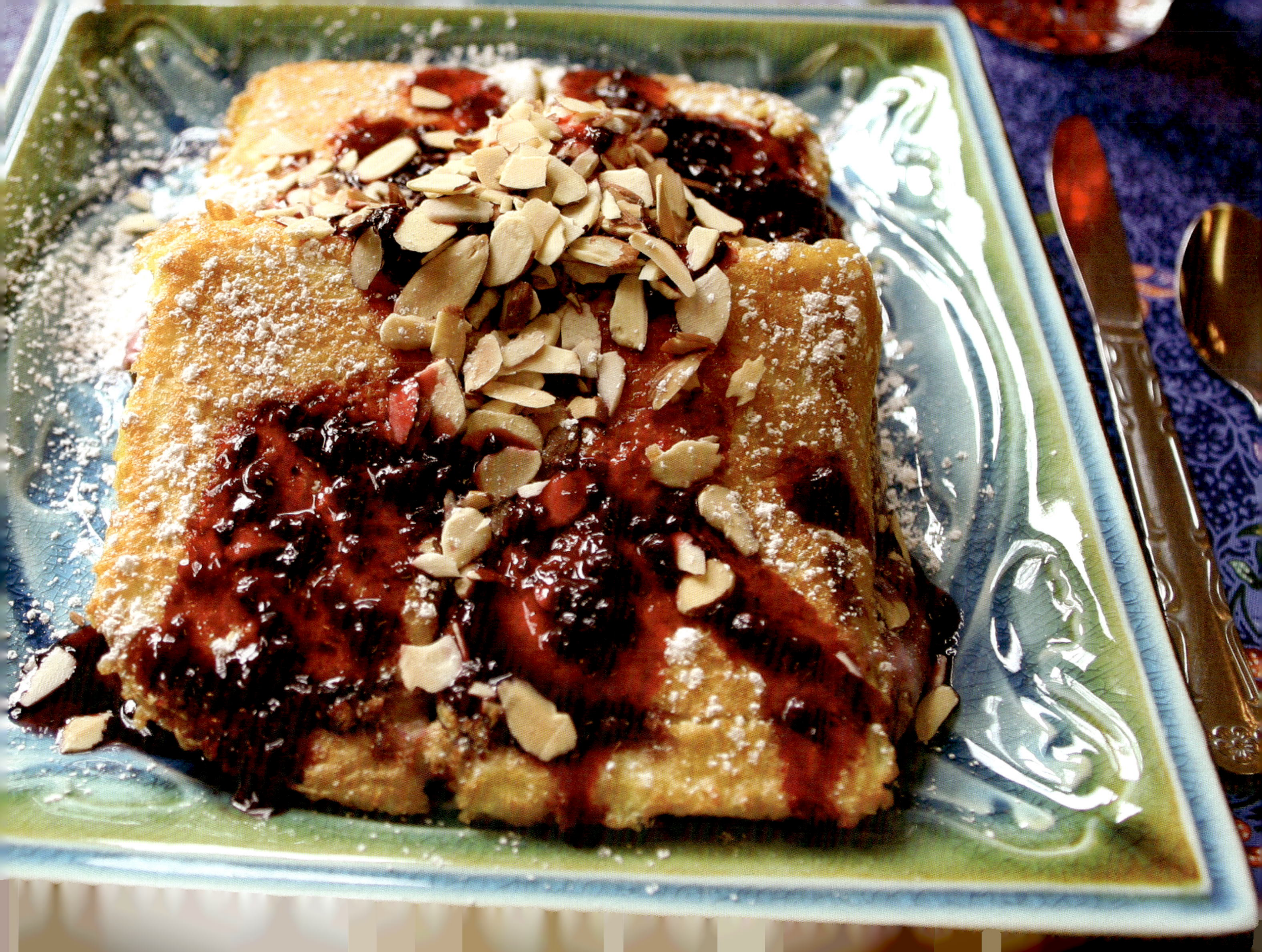

Marionberry Stuffed French Toast with Lemon Butter, Marionberry Syrup and Toasted Almonds

serves 4 to 6

Ingredients

1 recipe French Toast 101
24 ounces of cream cheese, softened to room temperature
2 cups Marionberries, fresh or frozen
2 cups sugar
2 teaspoons lemon zest, chopped
Lemon Butter (see recipe in The Finishing Touches section)
1 cup sliced almonds, toasted
1 Tablespoon of powdered sugar

1. In a mixer, combine cream cheese, Marionberries, sugar, lemon zest.

2. Take a large loaf of San Francisco Sourdough bread and use a large ice cream scoop to place cream cheese mixture in the middle of the bread. Using a knife, spread thoroughly. Top with another slice of bread and cut into thirds.

3. Dip bread into french toast batter and place on a heated griddle with a small amount of vegetable oil.

4. Cook until golden brown on both sides and the filling is heated.

Serve with lemon butter (see recipe in The Finishing Touches section), Marionberry syrup (see recipe in The Finishing Touches section), toasted almonds and sprinkle with powdered sugar.

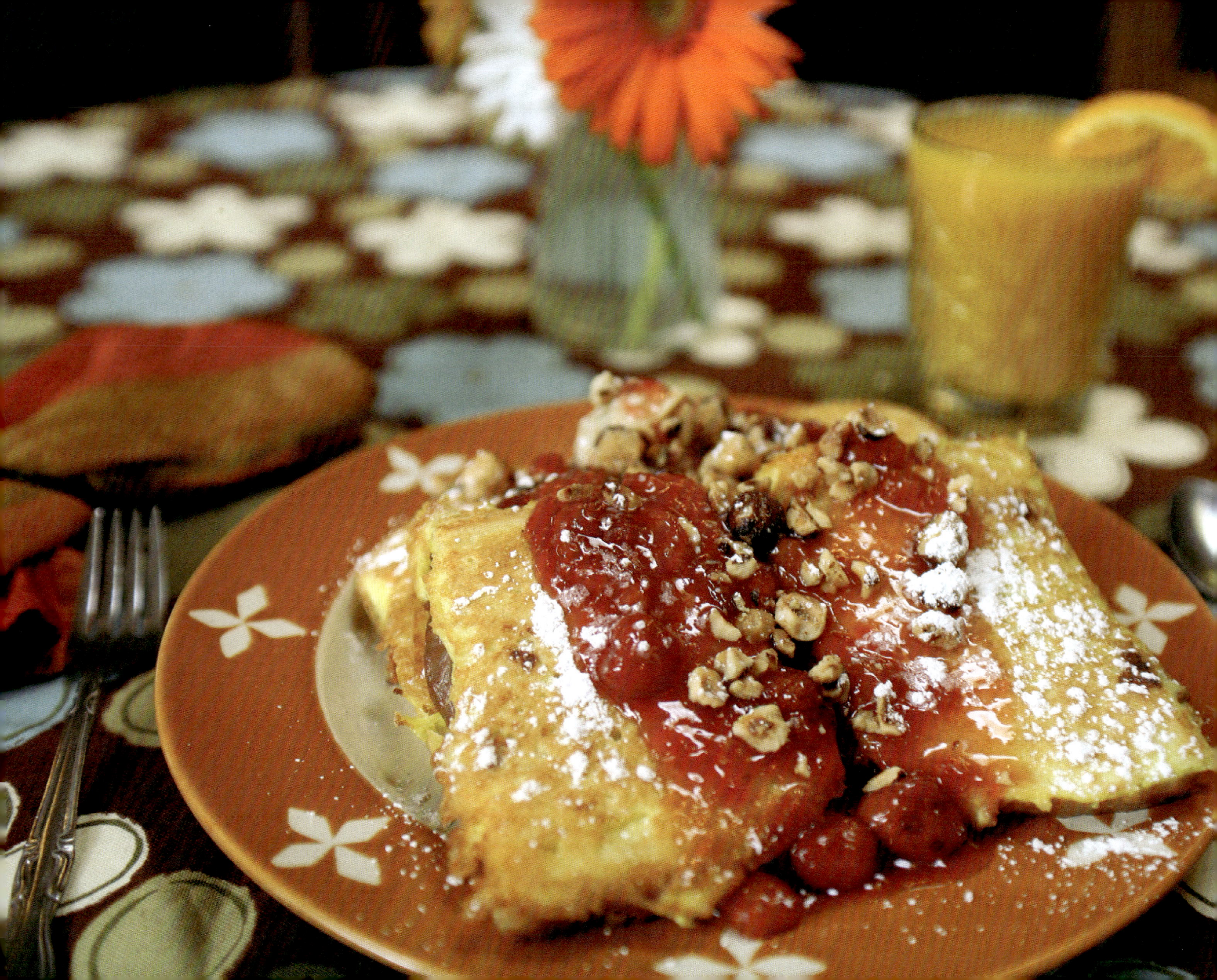

Nutella Stuffed French Toast with Amaretto Hazelnut Butter and Dark Cherry Syrup

serves 4 to 6

Ingredients

1 recipe French Toast 101
24 ounces of cream cheese, softened
1 13-ounce jar of Nutella Hazelnut Chocolate Spread
Powdered sugar

1. In a mixer, whip cream cheese until fluffy. Add the Nutella and whip until combined.

2. Use a large ice cream scoop to place cream cheese mixture in the center of one slice of sourdough bread; using a knife, spread thoroughly. Top with second slice of bread and cut the filled bread into thirds.

3. Dip into French Toast Batter and place on a heated griddle with a small amount of vegetable oil and butter.

4. Cook until the filling is heated and the bread is golden brown on both sides.

Serve with Amaretto Hazelnut Butter and Dark Cherry Syrup (see recipes in The Finishing Touch section) with a sprinkling of powdered sugar.

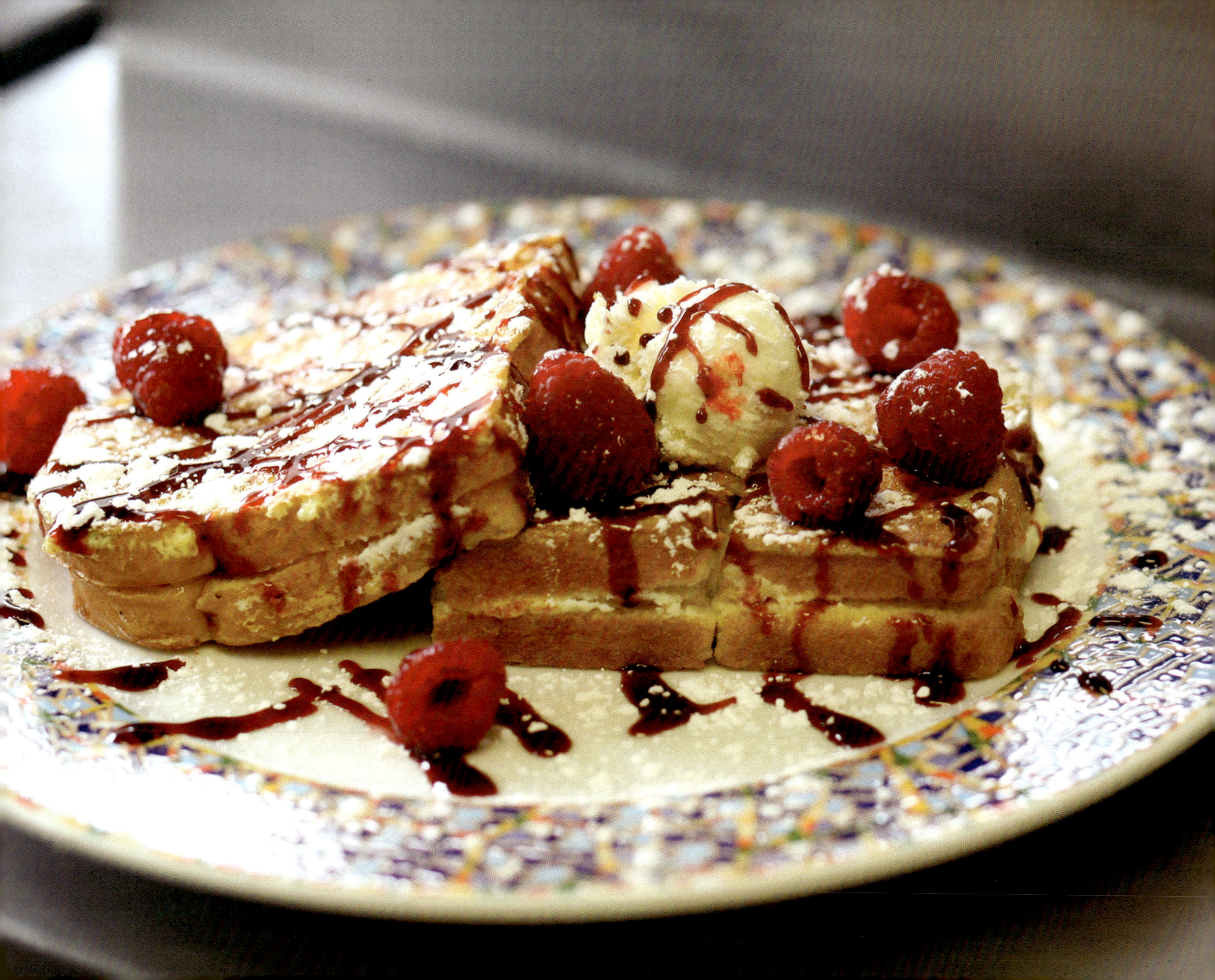

Lemon Ricotta French Toast with Lemon Butter and Raspberry Syrup

This is a signature dish at Morning Glory and has been on the menu for twenty-one years. I also served this at The McCully House Inn. It has been published and requested by Bon Apetit Magazine and other publications.
Perfect for a Sunday brunch for friends and family.

serves 4 to 6

Ingredients

1 recipe French Toast 101
2 15-ounce containers Ricotta cheese
1 cup sugar
Zest of one lemon, chopped

1. In a bowl combine the Ricotta cheese, sugar and lemon zest.

2. Use a large ice cream scoop to place cream cheese mixture on one slice of sourdough bread: using a knife, spread thoroughly. Top with second slice of bread and cut the filled bread into thirds. Repeat with other filling and slices.

3. Dip into French Toast Batter and place on a heated griddle with a small amount of vegetable oil.

4. Cook until the filling is heated and the bread is golden brown on both sides.

Top with Lemon Butter and Raspberry Syrup (See recipes in Finishing Touches section).

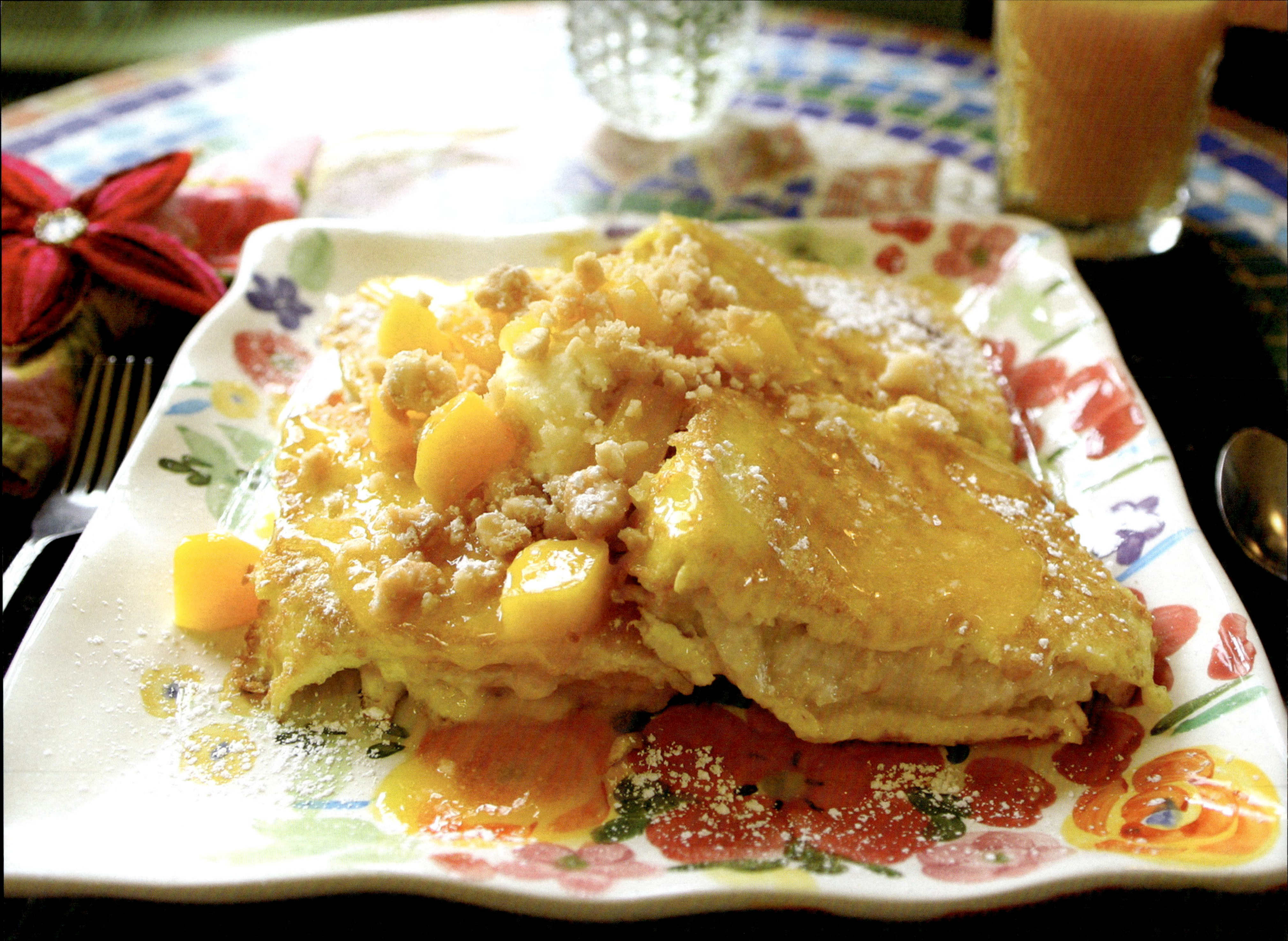

Coconut Cheesecake Stuffed French Toast with Lemon Butter, Mango Syrup and Macadamia Nuts

serves 4 to 6

Ingredients

1 recipe French Toast 101
24 ounces of cream cheese, softened
2 cups shredded coconut
2 cups sugar
2 teaspoons lemon zest, chopped
1 cup macadamia nuts, chopped
Powdered sugar

1. In a mixer, combine cream cheese, coconut, sugar and lemon zest

2. Use a large ice cream scoop to place cream cheese mixture in the middle of the bread. Using a knife, spread thoroughly. Top with another slice of bread and cut into thirds.

3. Dip bread into french toast batter and place on a heated griddle with a small amount of vegetable oil.

4. Cook until golden brown on both sides and the filling is hot.

Serve with Lemon Butter, Mango Syrup (see recipes in The Finishing Touches secton) and macadamia nuts and sprinkle with powdered sugar.

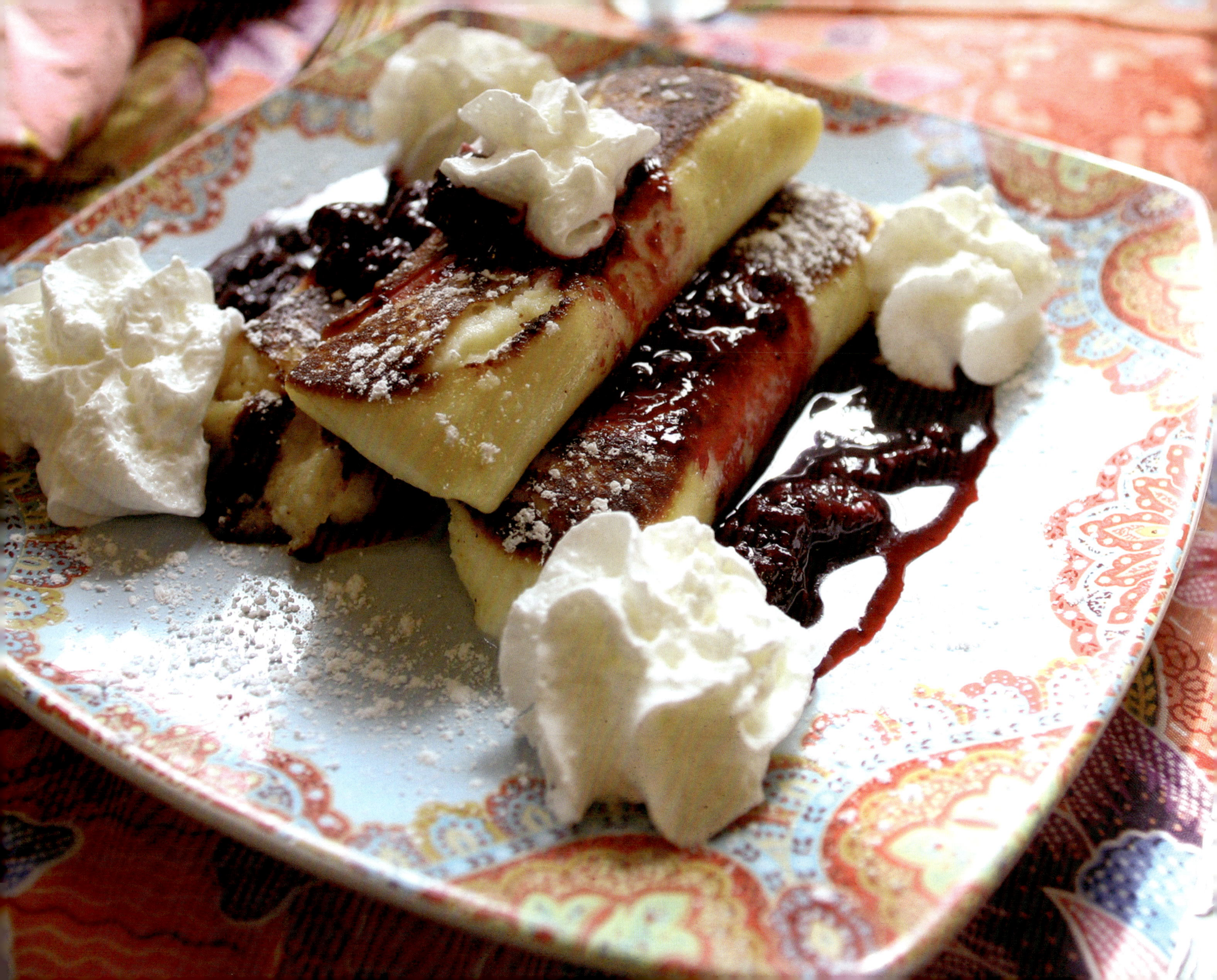

Cheese Blintzes with Whipped Cream and Marionberry Syrup

These are wonderful for a special occasion. You can even make the crepes and filling a day ahead. Just make sure to wrap the crepes carefully so that they don't dry out.

serves 4 to 6

Crepes
Ingredients

2 large eggs
1/2 cup milk
1/2 cup flour
2 large eggs
1/3 cup water
2 teaspoons vegetable oil
1/2 stick butter, cut into pieces

1. Combine crepe ingredients in a blender and then strain.

2. Let it rest for at least two hours or overnight before making crepes.

3. To make crepes, heat a 10-inch nonstick pan over low heat. Using a paper towel, spread a small amount of butter in the pan. Pour in a thin amount of batter and quickly rotate the pan to spread the batter evenly (takes some practice).

4. When the edges start to curl and brown, use your fingers or a thin spatula to flip the crepe over. Cook for about 30 seconds, then slide onto a sheet tray to cool. (Sometimes the first couple do not turn out. Just keep going and you will get the hang of it!) Do not stack the crepes until they are thoroughly cool.

5. Use immediately, or, if making ahead of time, stack and wrap airtight in plastic wrap to prevent drying out. (Can be refrigerated for up to 3 days, or frozen for weeks, but bring to room temperature before separating.) To use, fill with Ricotta cheese filling.

Ricotta Cheese Filling
Ingredients

4 cups Ricotta cheese
1/2 cup sugar
1 teaspoon lemon zest

Combine all above ingredients. Refrigerate if not using immediately.

Egg Wash
Ingredients

1 egg
1/2 cup of water

1. To fill the crepes, you will need a pastry brush and an egg wash.

2. Whisk together the egg with 1/2 cup of water. Lay the crepe flat and brush egg wash all the way around the edges.

3. Put 1/2 cup of filling lengthwise on the crepe. Fold in two edges and roll up tightly.

4. Place seam-side down on a plate and, if not cooking immediately, refrigerate up to 24 hours.

5. To cook, heat a large nonstick pan with a small amount of oil and butter. Place blintzes seam-side down over medium heat. Flip over when golden and continue cooking until filling is heated through and the crepes are golden brown.

Serve immediately with Marionberry Syrup (See recipe in Finishing Touches section), whipped cream, and powdered sugar.

Morning Glory: The Early Years

THE CULINARY INSTITUTE OF AMERICA

Graduation 1986 with President Ferdinand Metz

Phil and Patty

The Culinary Institute of America

I applied and was accepted at The Culinary Institute of America in Hyde Park, New York. I arrived in New York during the fall of 1984, to start the two-year program and vividly remember the profusion of fall colors, as I flew in a small plane to reach my final destination, Poughkeepsie.
I moved into a farmhouse in the country, nearby the school and got to work. I was terrified! I will never forget strolling down the long halls of the school to attend orientation and receive my knife kit, uniform and tall white paper hat. It felt a little like a military boot camp. Shoes had to be shined and your bright yellow neckerchief, perfectly knotted. This was a far cry from my customary cooking outfit of blue jeans and a baseball cap! Attending The CIA, during the early eighties was an exciting time. The whole food scene, especially in California, was exploding. America was finding it's own voice in the culinary world, incorporating fresh, local and seasonal ingredients.

The "farm to table" philosophy had begun and I started hearing names like Jeremiah Towers, Charlie Trotter, Alice Waters and Bradley Ogden, to name a few. Huge, wide-open kitchens with wood burning ovens, were the rage and were being designed to bring the cooking experience to the customer. As part of the curriculum, halfway through the program, we were expected to apply for a position in a prominent restaurant, anywhere in the United States or even Europe. Bradley Ogden had just been touted "Chef of the year" by Life magazine and I remember that there was a fullspread photo of him in a pile of carrots. I decided to apply at Campton Place Hotel on Union Square in San Francisco, where Bradley was the chef. I will never forget getting the interview phone call from Bradley, and stammering my way through the conversation trying to sound knowledgeable and using big words like "fresh"and "sourced" and "sustainable".
I had no idea what I was saying, I was so nervous, but at the end of the conversation,
he informed me that I was to report to duty, as soon as possible.
I hung up the phone and screamed!

It was thrilling to be back in San Francisco and at such an elegant hotel. I can remember how proud I felt when my parents came to the hotel for lunch, both working only a few blocks away.
It was at Campton Place Hotel that Bradley Ogden showed me a level of breakfast that I had never seen before. What a concept, I thought, to put breakfast on the same level as a gourmet dinner and he did it beautifully. I spent six months there and left with a job offer, if I so desired,
after graduation.

My original CIA textbook (still in use)
1984

Eggs and Others

Eggs and Others

Omelets 101   77
Pepper Seared Tri-Tip Omelet with Mushrooms, Spinach and Gorgonzola Cream   80

Poaching 101   81

Scrambles
Smoked Salmon, Yukon Potatoes, Red Onion and Lemon Dill Cream Scramble   84
Rainbow Swiss Chard, Pesto and Goat Cheese Scramble   86
Tofu Scramble with Carmelized Onion, Tomato, Kalamata Olive, Spinach, Feta and Parmesan   89
Tandoori Tofu Scramble with Sundried Cherry Cranberry Chutney, Peas and Toasted Almonds   90

Hashes
Beef Short Rib Hash with Poached Eggs and Fresh Horseradish Cream   92
Southwest Chorizo and Corn Hash with Poached Eggs and Orange Chipotle Hollandaise   94
Roasted Sweet Potato Hash with Poached Eggs and Lemon Thyme Cream   96
Southwest Smoked Chicken and Corn Hash with Chipotle Lime Hollandaise Sauce   98

Cakes
Rock Shrimp Cakes with Poached Eggs and Smoked Tomato Chutney   100
Masa Corn Cakes with Poached Eggs, Smoked Tomatillo Salsa and Cilantro Cream   102
Crispy Risotto Kale Cakes with Poached Eggs and Mushroom Gorganzola Cream Sauce   104

Others
Eggs Benedict with Black Forest Ham on Orange Cream Biscuit with Orange Hollandaise Sauce   106
Eggs Creole with Linguisa Sausage, Cheddar Grits and Remoulade Sauce   108
Huevos Rancheros with Black Beans, Tomatillo Sauce, Pepperjack, Cilantro Cream and Smoked Salsa   110

Omelet 101

Here at Morning Glory, our omelets are our best sellers. Omelets are a great way to use up leftovers as well.

1. To make an omelet: we crack, whisk, and then strain our eggs in order to remove the albumen and any shells that may have escaped.

2. Using a 10-inch non-stick, shallow frying pan, add about a tablespoon of vegetable oil to a cold pan, you may add an additional teaspoon of butter to make it richer. We then add a 6-ounce ladle of egg to the pan. It takes about 4 to 5 eggs (depending on size) per omelet, so adjust accordingly.

3. Turn on the heat and with a rubber spatula move the eggs around, lifting the edges and rotating the pan, let the liquid egg run underneath, so that all of the egg cooks evenly.

4. At this point, we flip the omelet over, add about 1 cup of filling, and roll onto a plate. We basically use a handful of each ingredient per omelet so I am not going to give you exact portions.

Omelet 101

Here is a sampling of some of our omelet fillings:

Chicken Basil Sausage, Portabella Mushrooms, Spinach, and Swiss Cheese

Slice chicken sausage into 1-inch rounds. Thinly slice the mushrooms and grate the Swiss cheese. Heat a frying pan with oil and butter. Add the sausages and mushrooms and sauté until the mushrooms are cooked. Add spinach, and when wilted, add the cheese. Season.

Tomato, Fresh Basil, and Smoked Mozzarella

Sometimes the simplest ingredients make the best omelets. This one is a winner, and is especially great when you use summer vine-ripened tomatoes. In a small skillet, over low heat, sauté some diced tomatoes in 1 tablespoon butter. Add chopped basil and grated smoked Mozzarella; cook until cheese is melted. Season.

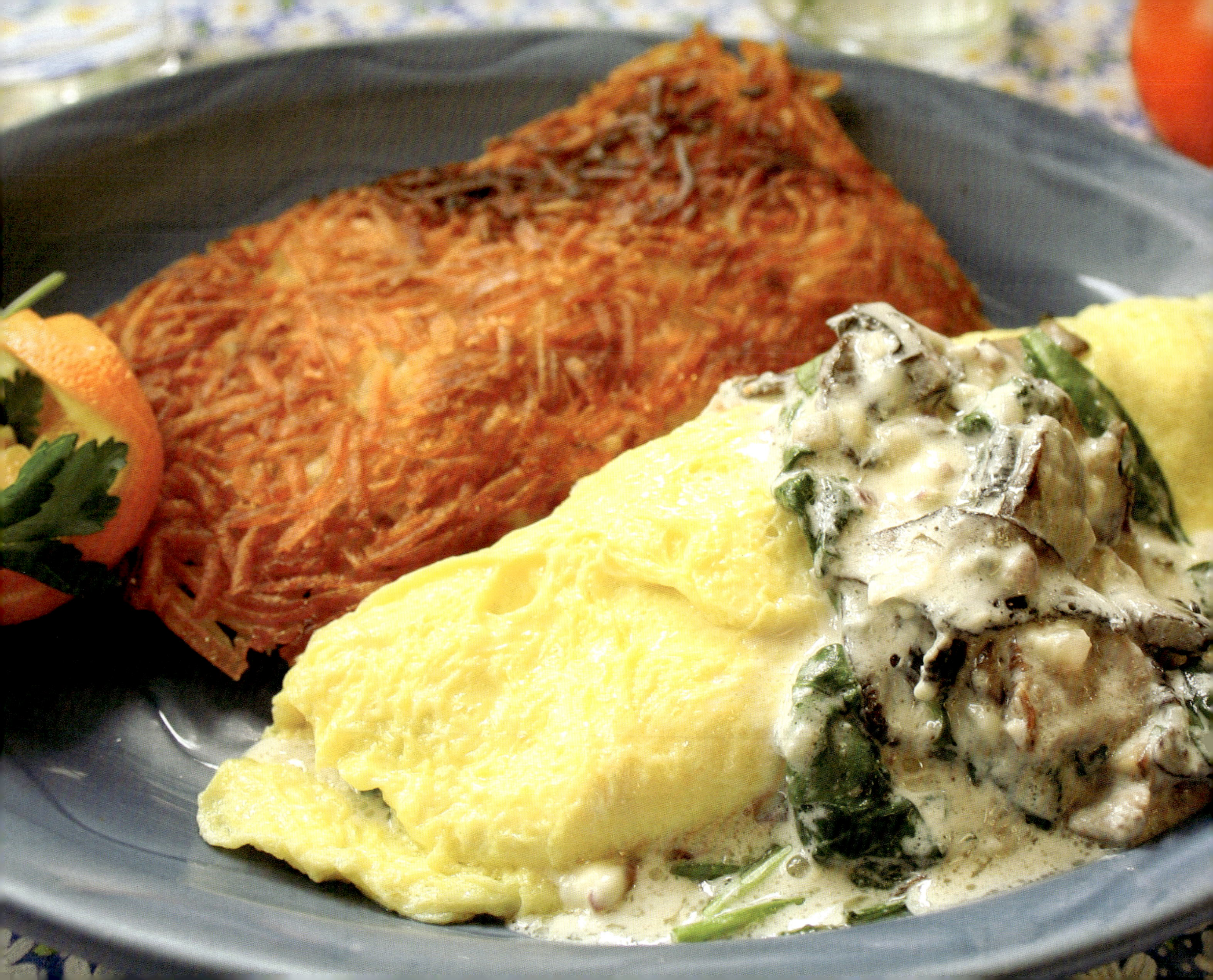

Pepper Seared Tri-Tip Omelet with Mushrooms, Spinach and Gorgonzola Cream

Wonderful for dinner with some oven-roasted potatoes and a glass of wine!

serves 4

Ingredients

1 to 2 pounds tri-tip steak
1/2 cup Worcestershire sauce
1/2 cup olive oil
1/2 cup minced garlic
Salt and pepper
2 cups sliced portabello or button mushrooms
1/2 cup minced red onion
1 Tablespoon each of butter and olive oil
1 pound raw spinach, rinsed
1 cup half and half
1/4 cup crumbled Gorgonzola cheese

1. The day before you make these omelets, marinate the steak overnight. Combine Worcestershire, olive oil, garlic, and salt and pepper in a large zip-lock bag, add the steak and refrigerate. (If you are in a pinch and can't marinate ahead of time, just salt and pepper the steak before searing. I highly recommend the extra step because it makes the omelet extra good.)

2. Heat some olive oil in a sauté pan until it starts to smoke. Carefully add the tri-tip and sear on both sides for about five minutes.

3. Remove meat from pan and let rest on a cutting board for 15 minutes to allow the juices to be absorbed. Thinly slice the steak. It will be rare.

4. Sauté mushrooms and onions in butter and oil. Add the spinach, half and half, and Gorgonzola; cook until the spinach is wilted and the cheese melted.

5. Add the steak and cook just until it reaches the desired doneness. (At the restaurant, I just toss the steak a few times in order to make it medium rare and heated through. The longer you cook it the tougher the steak will become.)

6. Cook omelet according to your liking and add filling, reserving a little for a garnish on top.

Egg Poaching 101

1. Fill a shallow skillet within a 1/4" to the top with water.

2. Add 1 tablespoon white vinegar and 1 tsp. salt

3. Bring the water just to a simmer.

4. Crack one egg at a time into a small bowl and gently slip it into the water. (This way, you can discard any egg shells or bad eggs.)

5. Using a slotted spoon, lift an egg out of the water and use your finger to test for doneness. Soft eggs take approximately 2 minutes; medium eggs, 4 minutes; hard eggs, as long as you like!

6. Drain well, and enjoy on buttered toast, or atop one of our many poached egg recipes.

82

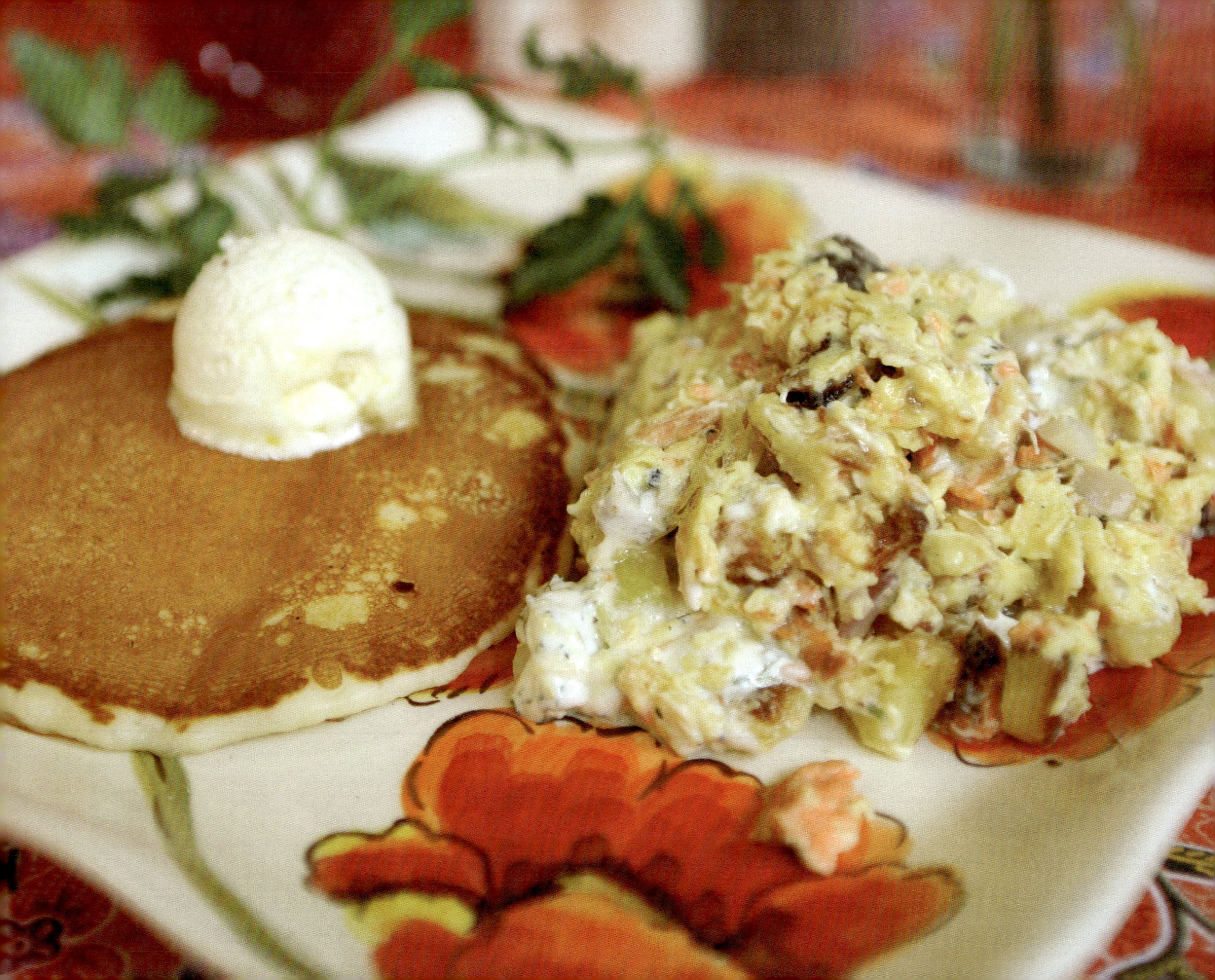

Smoked Salmon, Yukon Gold Potatoes, Red Onion and Lemon Dill Sour Cream Scramble

At Morning Glory, we have a smoker in back where we get massive deliveries of various hardwoods depending on what is available. We smoke everything from garlic to salmon, duck, chicken, pork, and our salsa and chutney ingredients.

If you don't have a smoker or are short on time, purchase smoked salmon from your grocery store. To smoke your own salmon, purchase one full wild salmon filet, skin on or off from the fishmonger. Get your smoker going, season filet with salt and pepper, and place in smoker skin side down. Lower the lid and smoke until firm to the touch and golden. Cool the salmon and scrape off any grey flesh. Using your fingers, gently flake salmon, checking for any hidden bones.

serves 4

Ingredients

2 cups flaked smoked salmon
1 small red onion
6 Yukon gold potatoes
1 dozen eggs

1. Cook the potatoes in salted water until tender. Cool and cut into small dice.

2. Mince the red onion. Crack, whisk, and strain the eggs.

3. Heat a large sauté pan with some vegetable oil.

4. Add the potatoes and cook until golden brown, seasoning with salt and pepper.

5. Add the salmon and onion and heat through. Stir in the eggs; scramble until set.

6. Fold in the Lemon Dill Cream.

Lemon Dill Cream

Ingredients

1 cup sour cream
3 Tablespoons lemon juice
1 Tablespoon minced garlic
1 bunch of fresh dill, finely chopped

Combine the sour cream, the garlic, lemon juice and minced dill.

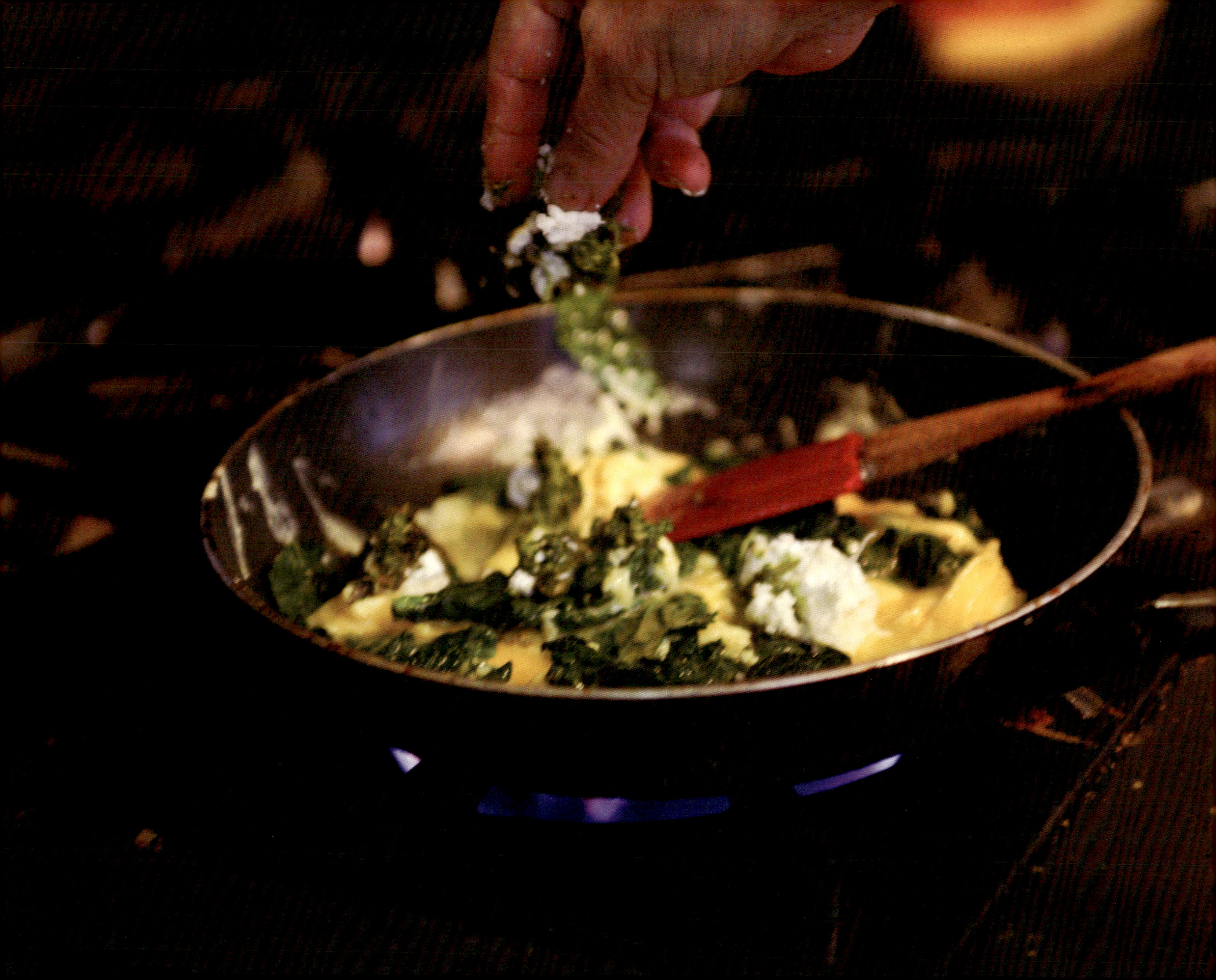

Rainbow Swiss Chard, Pesto and Goat Cheese Scramble

This scramble is delicious for breakfast, or serve with a salad and you have lunch or dinner! We make this with Basil Pesto (see recipe in The Finishing Touches section) but you could easily substitute cilantro or parsley for a different twist.

serves 2 to 4

Ingredients

1 bunch Swiss chard
1 dozen eggs
1 tablespoon butter
1 tablespoon olive oil
1/2 cup Pesto (See Finishing Touches section)
1/2 cup goat cheese, crumbled

1. Start by bringing a large pot of salted water to a boil. Devein the chard by pulling out and discarding the center vein, which is tough. Carefully drop the chard into the water to blanch it for 3 minutes. Drain and rinse with cold water, squeezing out excess water with your hands. Chop coarsely, set aside.

2. Crack and whisk the eggs and then strain the eggs through a sieve. (This process removes any egg shells and the albumen.)

3. In a large non-stick pan, melt butter and oil on low heat. Add chard and heat through. Add the eggs and gently stir with a rubber spatula. When eggs are almost cooked, blend in Pesto and Goat cheese.

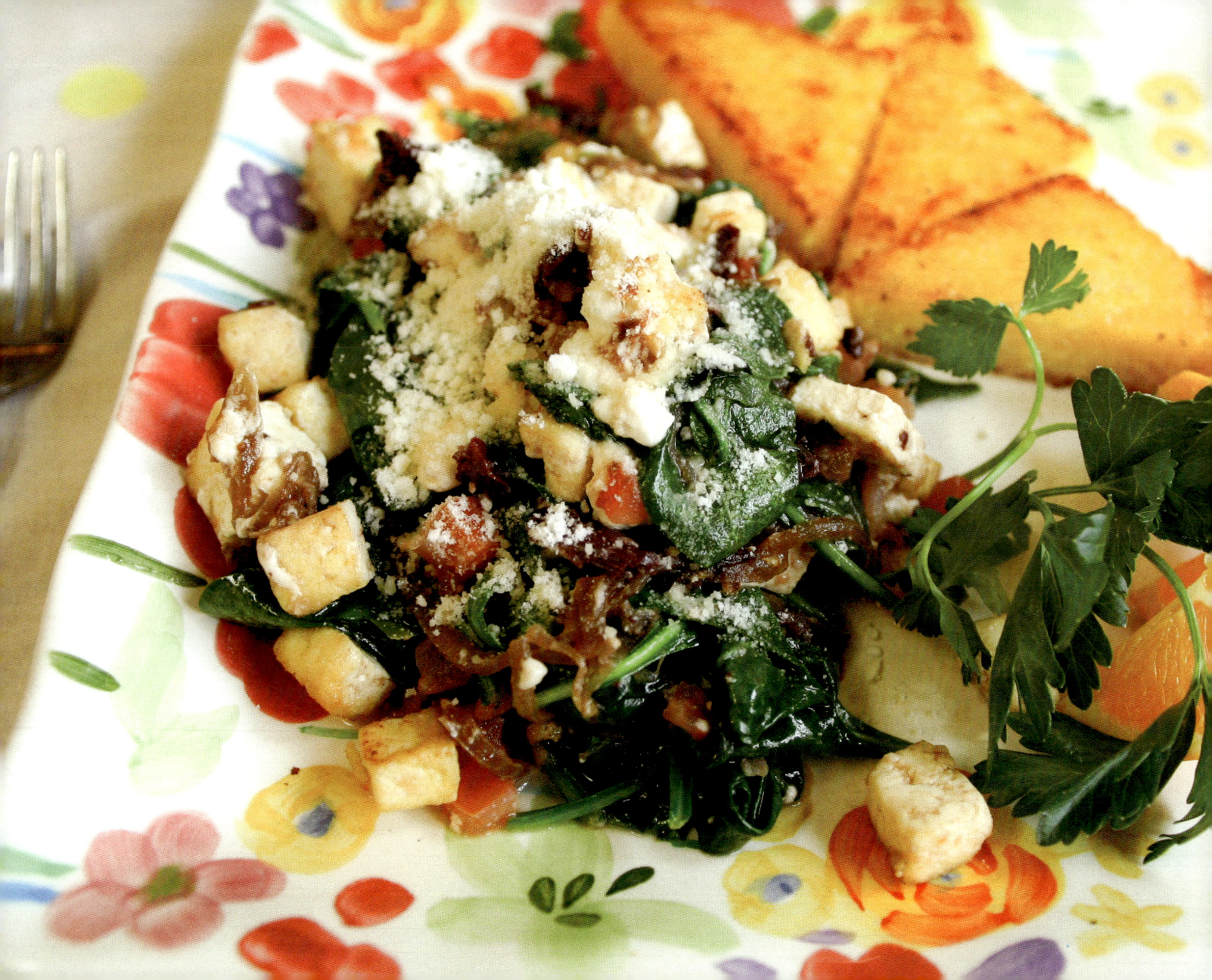

Tofu Scramble with Caramelized Onion, Tomato, Kalamata Olive, Spinach, Feta and Parmesan

serves 2 to 4

Ingredients

2 pounds firm (organic) tofu, drained, and diced or crumbled
1/2 cup Caramelized Onions (See recipe in Finishing Touches section)
1 tomato, diced
1/2 cup chopped Kalamata olives
1 pound spinach, rinsed and squeezed dry
1 cup Feta cheese, crumbled
1/2 cup grated Parmesan cheese

1. Drain and dice or crumble tofu.

2. In a large skillet, add 2 tablespoons vegetable oil over high heat. When hot, add the tofu and cook, stirring, until golden brown.

3. Add Caramelized Onion, tomato and olives, and cook for one minute.

4. Add spinach and Feta and cook just until wilted. Top with grated Parmesan and serve.

Bev

Lee

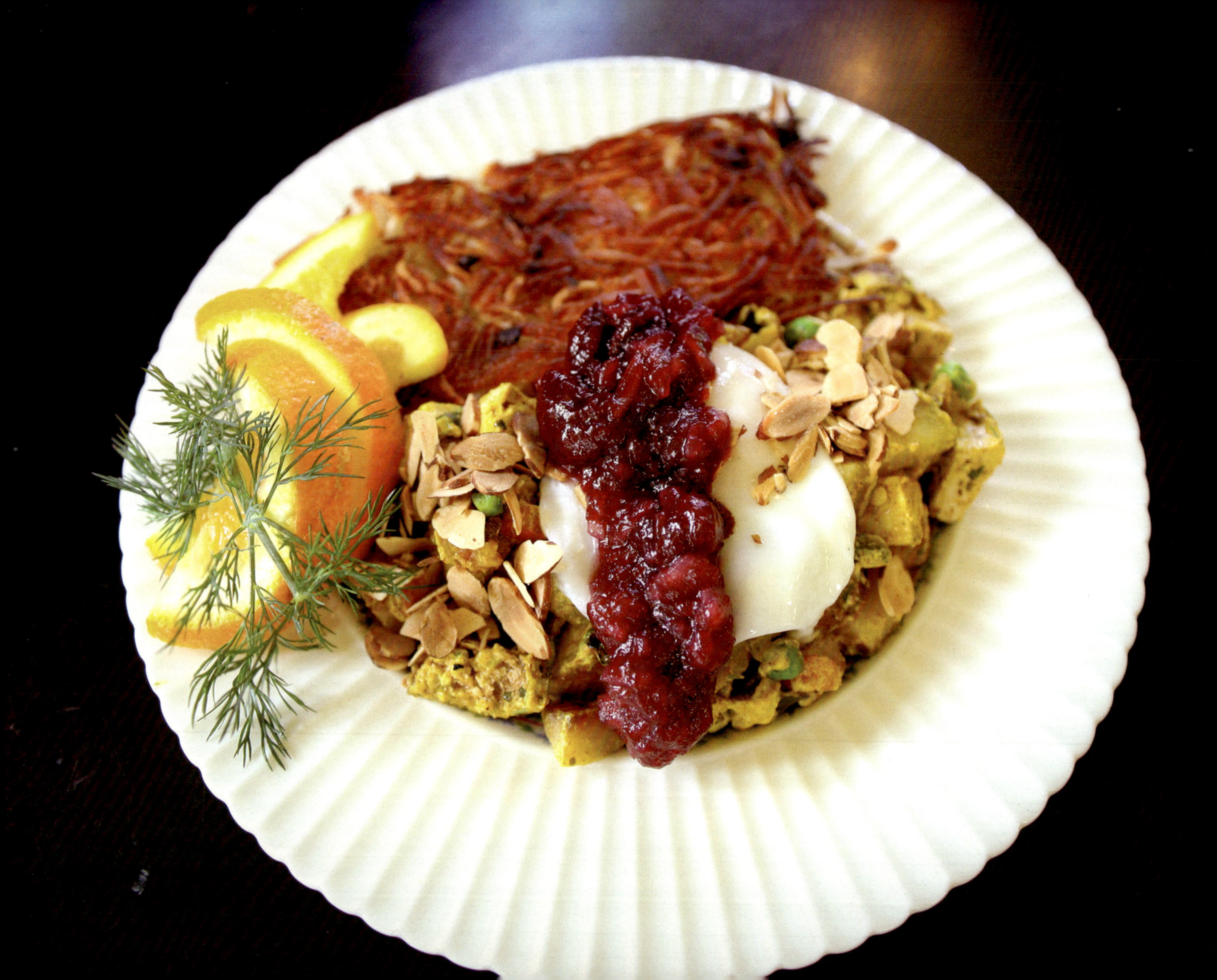

Tandoori Tofu Scramble Sun-dried Cherry Cranberry Chutney, Peas and Toasted Almonds

serves 2 to 4

Ingredients
2 (14 ounce) packages of firm organic tofu, drained

Tofu Marinade

1/2 cup olive oil
1/4 cup brown sugar
2 Tablespoons curry powder
1 Tablespoon minced garlic
1 teaspoon ground ginger
1/8 teaspoon ground cloves
Salt and pepper, to taste

1. In a baking pan that will just fit the tofu, combine olive oil, brown sugar, garlic and spices with a whisk. Add tofu, coating both sides, refrigerate and marinate overnight.

2. Bake at 300 degrees until golden and puffy, approximately 2 hours.

3. Chill and cut into small to medium dice.

Curry Yogurt

1 cup plain yogurt
3 Tablespoons dried currants
1 teaspoon ground cumin
1 teaspoon ground turmeric
1 teaspoon curry powder
1 teaspoon brown sugar
1 teaspoon minced garlic
Salt and pepper, to taste

Combine and refrigerate for an hour or more to let flavors blend.

To Assemble:

3 medium Yukon gold potatoes
1/2 cups frozen peas
1 cup sliced almonds, toasted

1. Cook potatoes in salted water until tender. Cool and cut into medium dice.

2. Heat a large skillet with a tablespoon or so of vegetable oil, add the potatoes.

3. Stir in the Tandoori tofu and Curry Yogurt. When heated through, add the peas and cook for one minute (until just thawed).

Top with Sun-Dried Cherry Cranberry Chutney (see recipe in The Finishing Touches section) and toasted almonds.

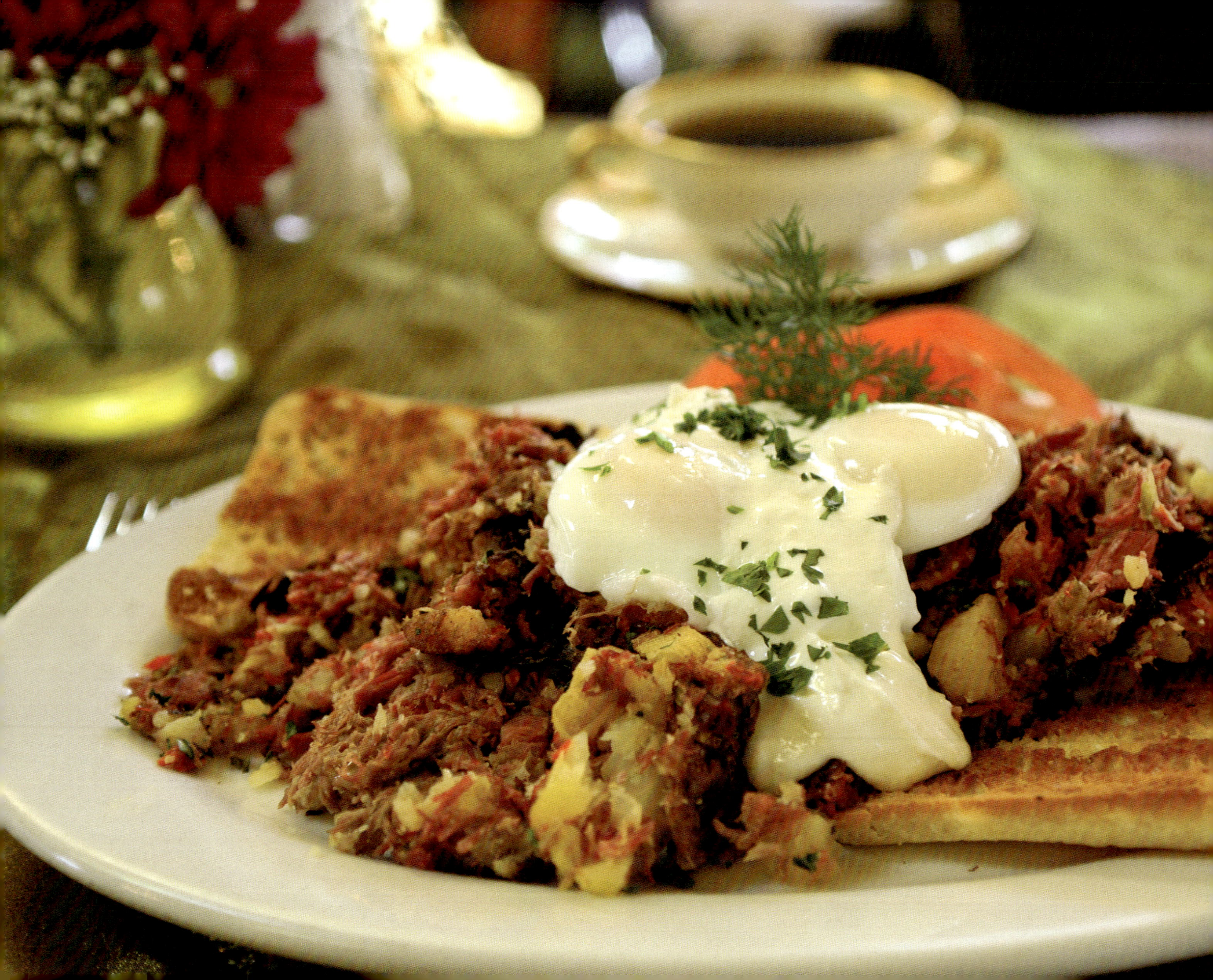

Beef Short Rib Hash with Poached Eggs and Fresh Horseradish Cream

serves 4-6

Ingredients

10 pounds beef short ribs
¼ cup vegetable oil
8 cups (2 quarts) canned beef broth
8 Yukon gold potatoes
1 Tablespoon each butter and vegetable oil
2 red bell peppers, seeded and diced
2 green bell peppers, seeded and diced
2 yellow onions, chopped
¼ cup (4 tablespoons) minced garlic
1 bunch fresh thyme, chopped
1 bunch fresh Italian parsley, chopped
12 poached eggs

1. In a large sauté pan, heat vegetable oil until smoking. Carefully, sear ribs on both sides, seasoning with salt and pepper. Place in a deep, oven-proof pan and pour in beef broth. Cover pan with foil and braise ribs in a 300-degree oven until tender (approximately 3 to 4 hours).

2. Set aside, and when cool enough to handle, use fingers to remove meat in bite size pieces, discarding fat and bones.
(You can save the rich broth for soup—just freeze for another day.)

3. While the beef is braising, add potatoes to a large saucepot with salt and enough cold water to cover. Boil until tender, drain and chill with cold water, dice, and set aside.

4. In a skillet, melt butter and oil. Sauté peppers and onions, and as they soften, add the garlic. When nice and soft, add chopped parsley and thyme. Set aside to cool.

5. To finish the hash, combine shredded meat, potatoes and pepper/onion mix in a large bowl.

6. For one serving, heat a skillet, preferably non-stick, with vegetable oil. When oil is hot, add 2 to 3 cups hash, season with salt and pepper, and cook until crispy on both sides.

Top with poached eggs and Horseradish Cream (see recipe in The Finishing Touch section).

The fabulous artwork by Suzanne Ettienne which adorns every wall in Morning Glory

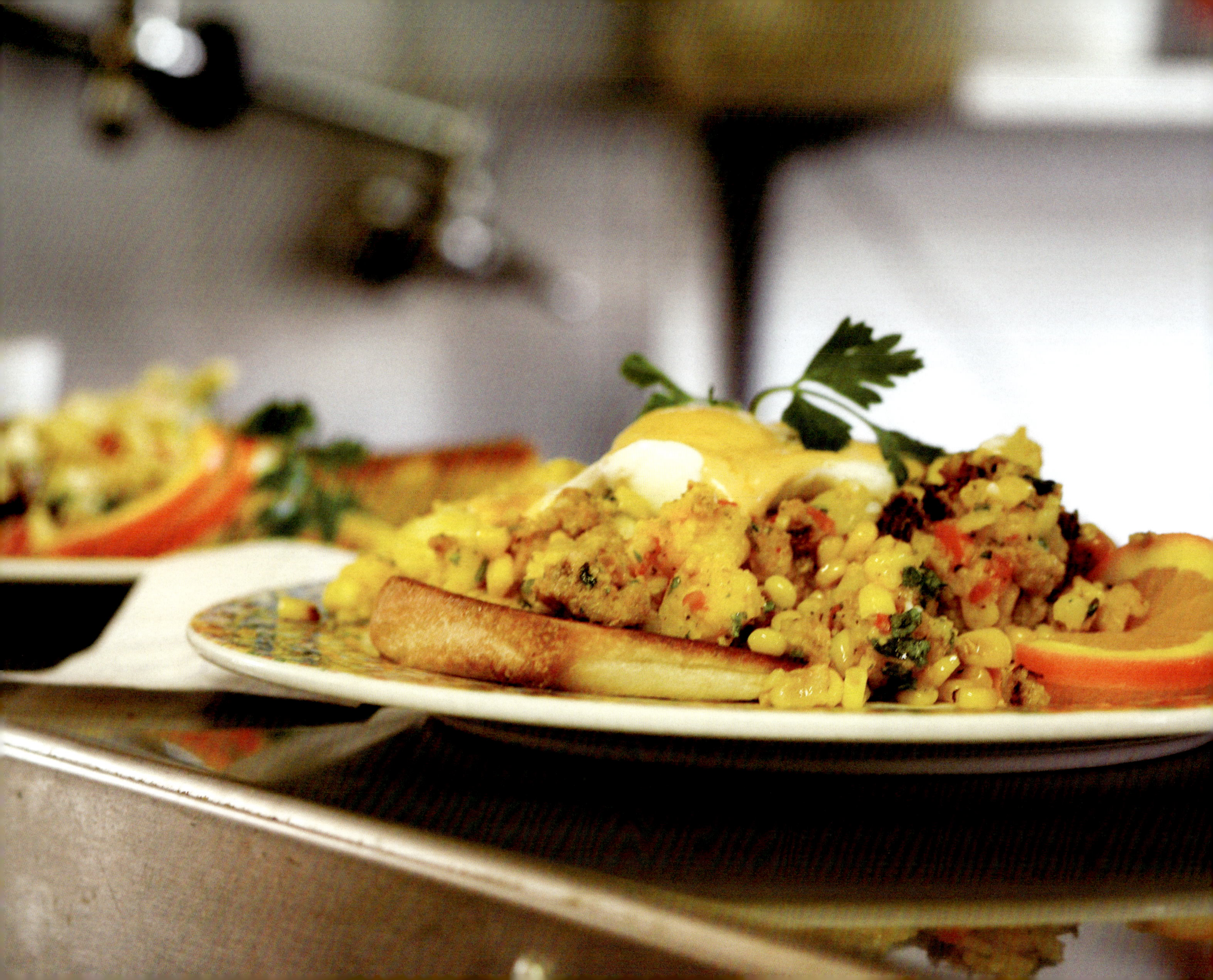

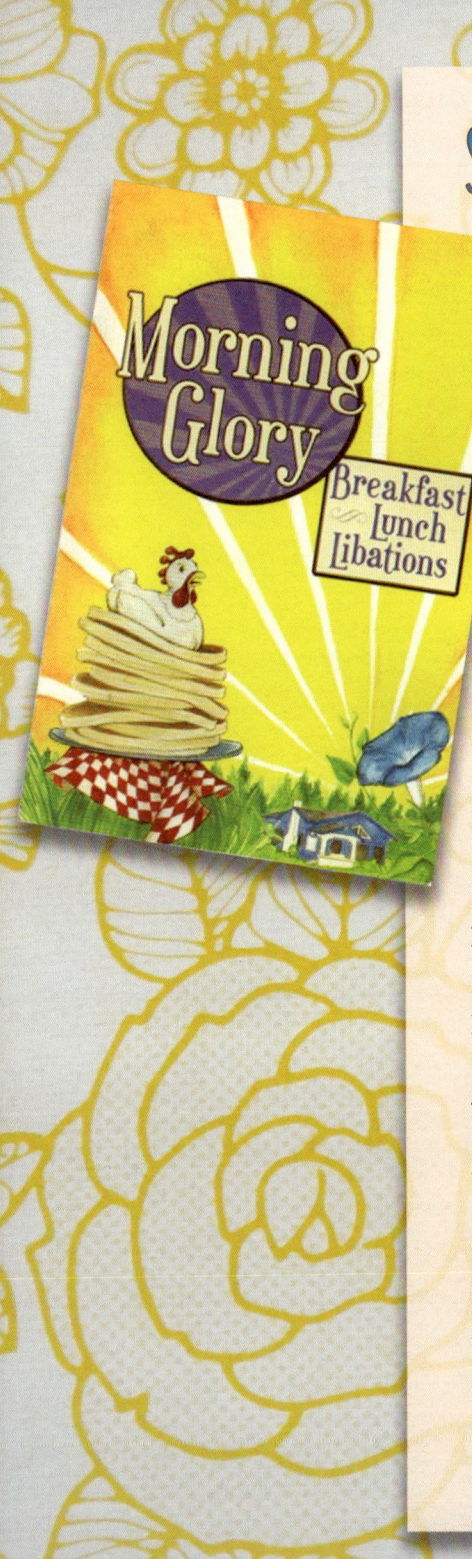

Southwestern Chorizo and Corn Hash with Poached Eggs and Orange Chipotle Hollandaise

Great in summertime with fresh corn purchased at a farm stand.
Delicious in wintertime as well, when you substitute frozen corn.
We use a drier form of chorizo than is usually found in a grocery store,
a brand called "Rose's Chorizo" that can be purchased online at
www.rosepacking.com/shop/.
You can use supermarket chorizo if you drain it well.

serves 6

Ingredients

2 pounds Yukon gold potatoes
2 pounds chorizo
1 yellow onion, finely diced
1 red onion, finely diced
1 jalapeno pepper, seeded and minced
1/4 cup minced garlic

2 Tablespoons chili powder
2 Tablespoons ground cumin
1 bunch cilantro, chopped including stems
4 ears fresh corn
12 poached eggs
3 cups Orange Chipotle Hollandaise (See The Finishing Touches section)

1. Place potatoes in a large saucepot with salt and enough cold water to cover.
Boil until tender, chill with cold water, dice, and set aside.

2. Crumble the chorizo into a medium saucepan and cook until golden brown.
Drain the fat into a skillet, set it aside, and reserve the chorizo.

3. In the chorizo fat, sauté the jalapeno and onions, and as they soften, add the garlic.
When nice and soft, add the spices and fresh cilantro and cook for two minutes to release the flavors.

4. Shuck the fresh corn and cut off the kernels. Add to the onion/pepper mixture.

5. To finish the hash, add the diced potatoes and crumbled chorizo to the vegetable mixture.
Season with salt and pepper.

6. For one serving, heat a medium skillet, preferably non-stick, with vegetable oil.
When oil is hot, add 2 to 3 cups hash, season with salt and pepper, and cook until
crispy on both side.

Top hash with poached eggs and Orange Chipotle Hollandaise (See The Finishing Touches section).

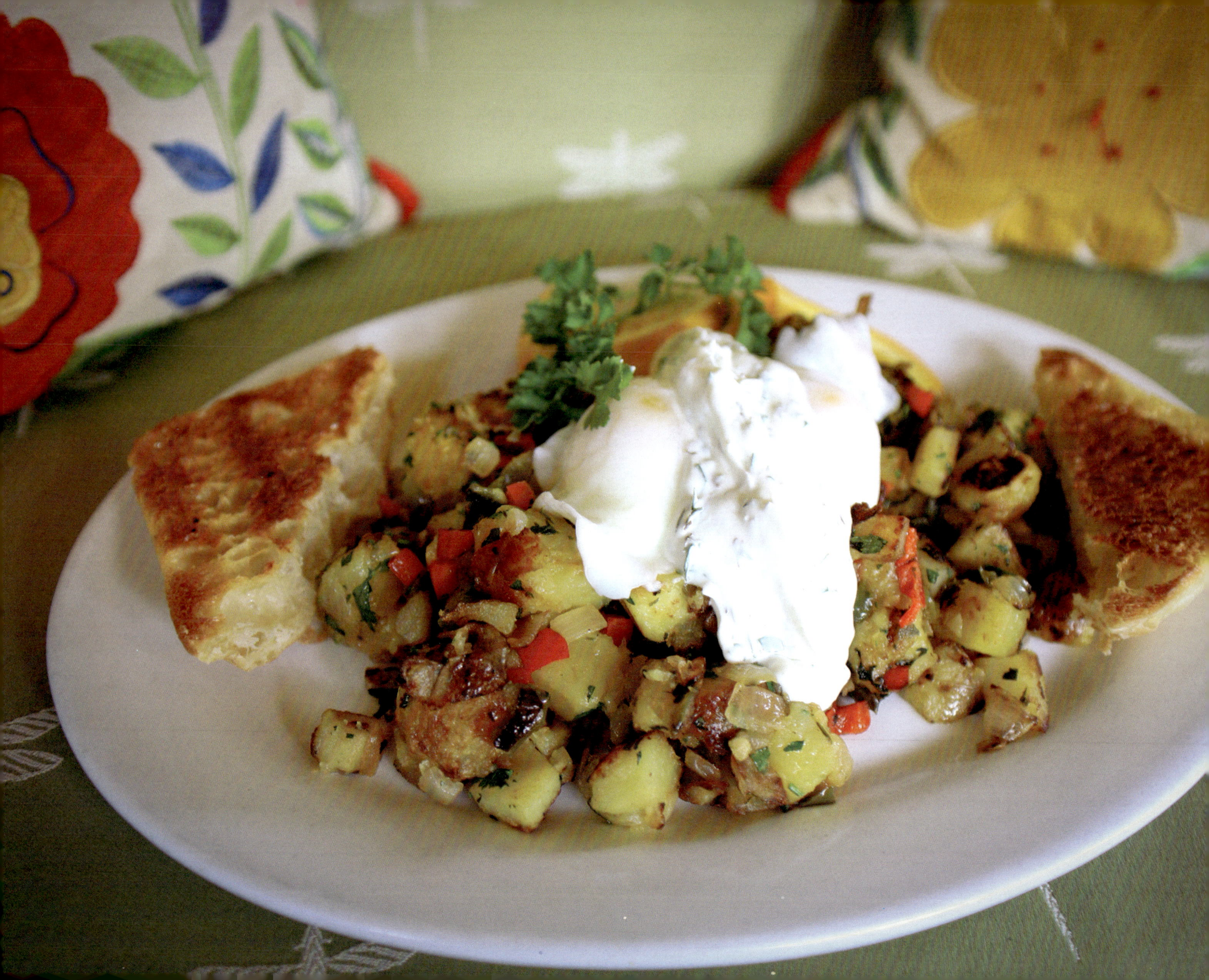

Roasted Sweet Potato Hash with Poached Eggs and Lemon Thyme Cream

This vegetarian hash was on our menu for a few years and was very popular. It would be the perfect Thanksgiving day brunch entrée, or even the day after with some turkey added to it for a meat version.

serves 6

Ingredients

- 6 large sweet potatoes, rubbed with olive oil
- 6 medium Yukon gold potatoes
- 2 Tablespoons each butter and vegetable oil
- 2 yellow onions, finely diced
- 2 red peppers, chopped
- 2 fresh Poblano peppers
- 1 Tablespoon minced garlic
- 2 Tablespoons minced fresh thyme leaves
- 2 Tablespoon minced fresh parsley
- Salt and pepper, to taste
- 12 poached eggs
- Lemon Thyme Cream

1. Place the oiled sweet potatoes on a sheet tray and roast in a 350 degree oven until tender but not overcooked, approximately 30 to 40 minutes. Cool, peel and cut into medium dice.

2. Cook the Yukon potatoes in salted water until tender; drain, cool and dice.

3. Place Poblano peppers, place on a sheet tray in a 400-degree oven with a small amount of oil until the skin is black and blistered. Place them in a plastic bag and seal; set aside to steam and cool. Wearing gloves, peel off the charred skin and rinse out the seeds. Dice.

4. In a large sauté pan, heat butter and oil and add the onions; cook until soft.

5. To finish the hash, add the sweet potatoes, potatoes, peppers, garlic and herbs and season well with salt and pepper.

6. For one serving, heat a medium skillet, preferably non-stick, with vegetable oil. When oil is hot, add 2 to 3 cups hash and cook until crispy on both sides and golden brown.

Top with poached eggs and a dollop of Lemon Thyme Cream.

Lemon Thyme Cream

Ingredients

- 2 cups sour cream
- 2 Tablespoons lemon juice
- 2 Tablespoons minced garlic
- 2 Tablespoons fresh thyme leaves, minced

Combine ingredients; season to taste. Refrigerate to allow flavors to blend.

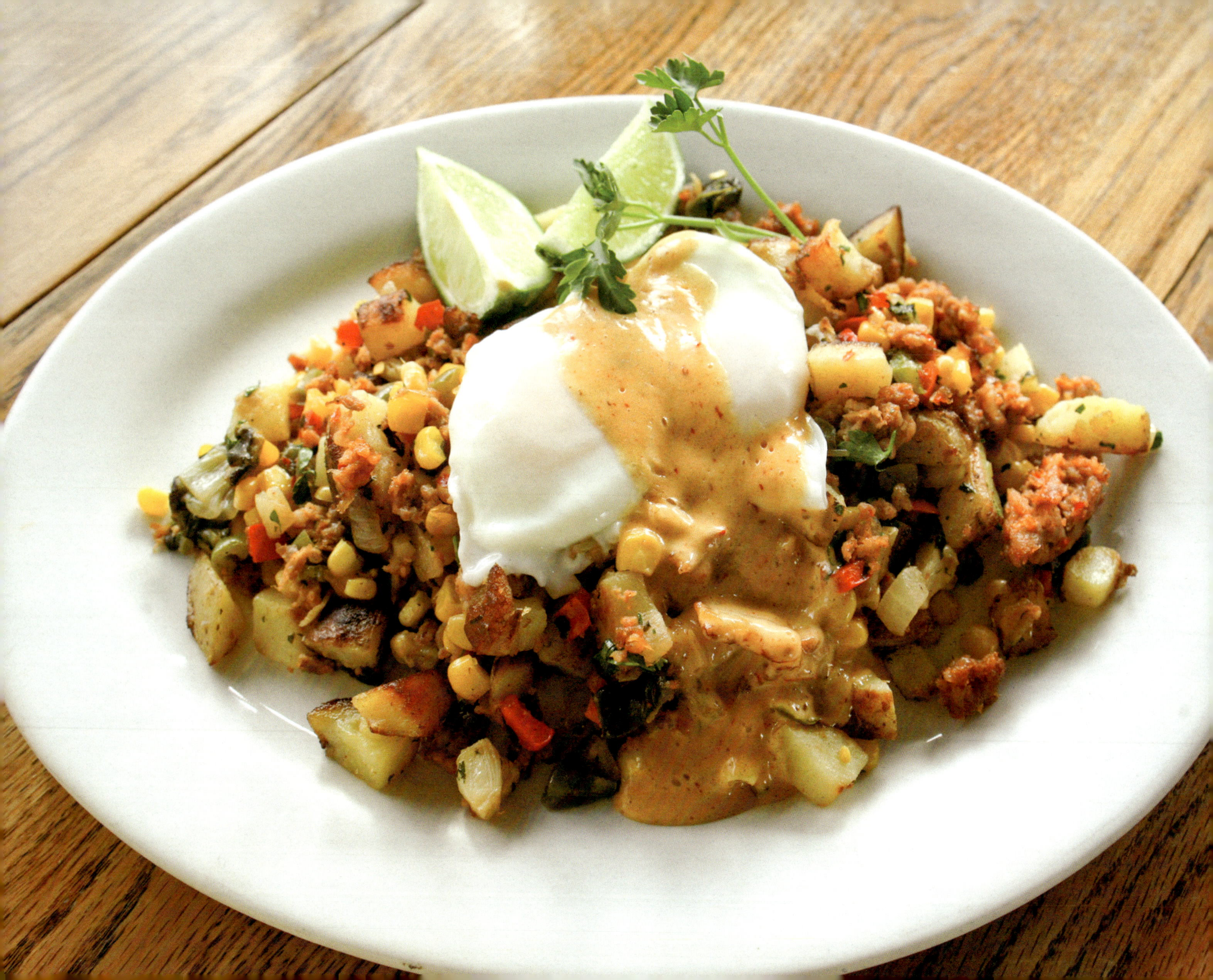

Southwestern Smoked Chicken and Corn Hash with Chipotle Lime Hollandaise Sauce

This hash is great for a weekend brunch for friends and family. I like to smoke the chicken and cook the potatoes the day before. You can also sauté the peppers and onions ahead of time, so this dish is just a quick, last-minute assembly. Well worth the effort!

serves 6

Ingredients

6 skinless and boneless chicken breast halves
6 Yukon gold potatoes
1 red bell pepper, seeded and diced
1 green bell pepper, seeded and diced
1 yellow onion, chopped
1/4 cup minced garlic
1 Tablespoon ground chili powder
1 Tablespoon ground cumin
4 ears of fresh corn
1 bunch cilantro, chopped including stems
Salt and pepper to taste
12 poached eggs
Chipotle Lime Hollandaise Sauce (See recipe in Finishing Touches)

1. Smoke the chicken breasts in a smoker until just barely cooked; cool and dice.

2. Cook the potatoes in salted water until tender; drain, chill, dice.

3. In a skillet, sauté the peppers and onion until soft; add the garlic and spices and cook for one minute longer. Cool.

4. Shuck the corn and remove the kernels; add to the onion/pepper mixture.

5. Finish hash by adding cilantro and diced chicken.

6. For one serving, heat a medium skillet, preferably non-stick, with vegetable oil. When oil is hot, add 2 to 3 cups hash and cook until crispy on both sides and golden brown. Season to taste.

Top with poached eggs and Hollandaise Sauce.

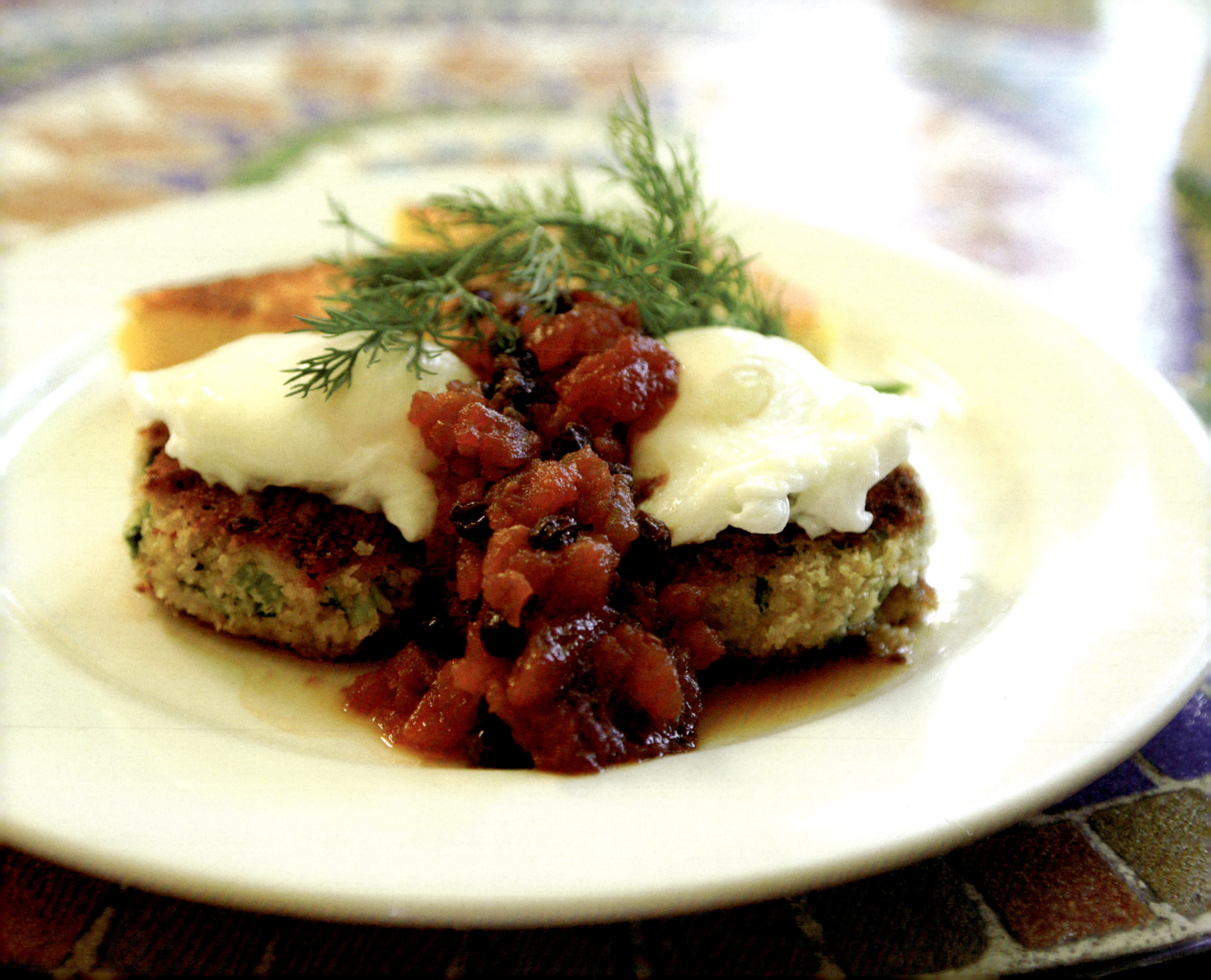

Shrimp Cakes with Poached Eggs and Smoked Tomato Chutney

These are a signature item at Morning Glory.
The Tomato Chutney lends a smoky, sweet complement.

serves 6

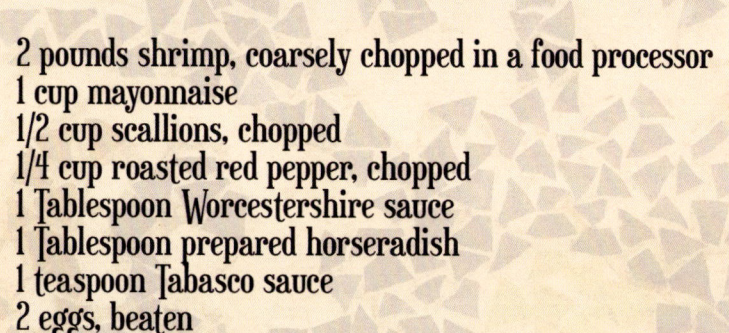

Ingredients

2 pounds shrimp, coarsely chopped in a food processor
1 cup mayonnaise
1/2 cup scallions, chopped
1/4 cup roasted red pepper, chopped
1 Tablespoon Worcestershire sauce
1 Tablespoon prepared horseradish
1 teaspoon Tabasco sauce
2 eggs, beaten
Salt and pepper, to taste
4 cups Panko breadcrumbs, divided

Vegetable oil or olive oil for browning
12 eggs for poaching

1. Preheat oven to 350 degrees.

2. Combine shrimp cake ingredients with 2 cups of the breadcrumbs in a large bowl. Let set for 20 minutes to allow the breadcrumbs to absorb the liquid.

3. Place the other 2 cups breadcrumbs into a bowl. Form the shrimp mixture into 3-inch cakes. Dip one at a time into the remaining crumbs to lightly bread the outside of the cakes.

4. In a large skillet, heat enough oil to cover the bottom. Add the shrimp cakes and when golden brown, flip to the other side. Arrange on a baking sheet and place in the oven to finish cooking (approximately 8 minutes).

While they are cooking, poach your eggs to desired firmness and heat the Smoked Tomato Chutney (see recipe in The Finishing Touch section). On serving plates, top two shrimp cakes with two poached eggs and garnish with Smoked Tomato Chutney.

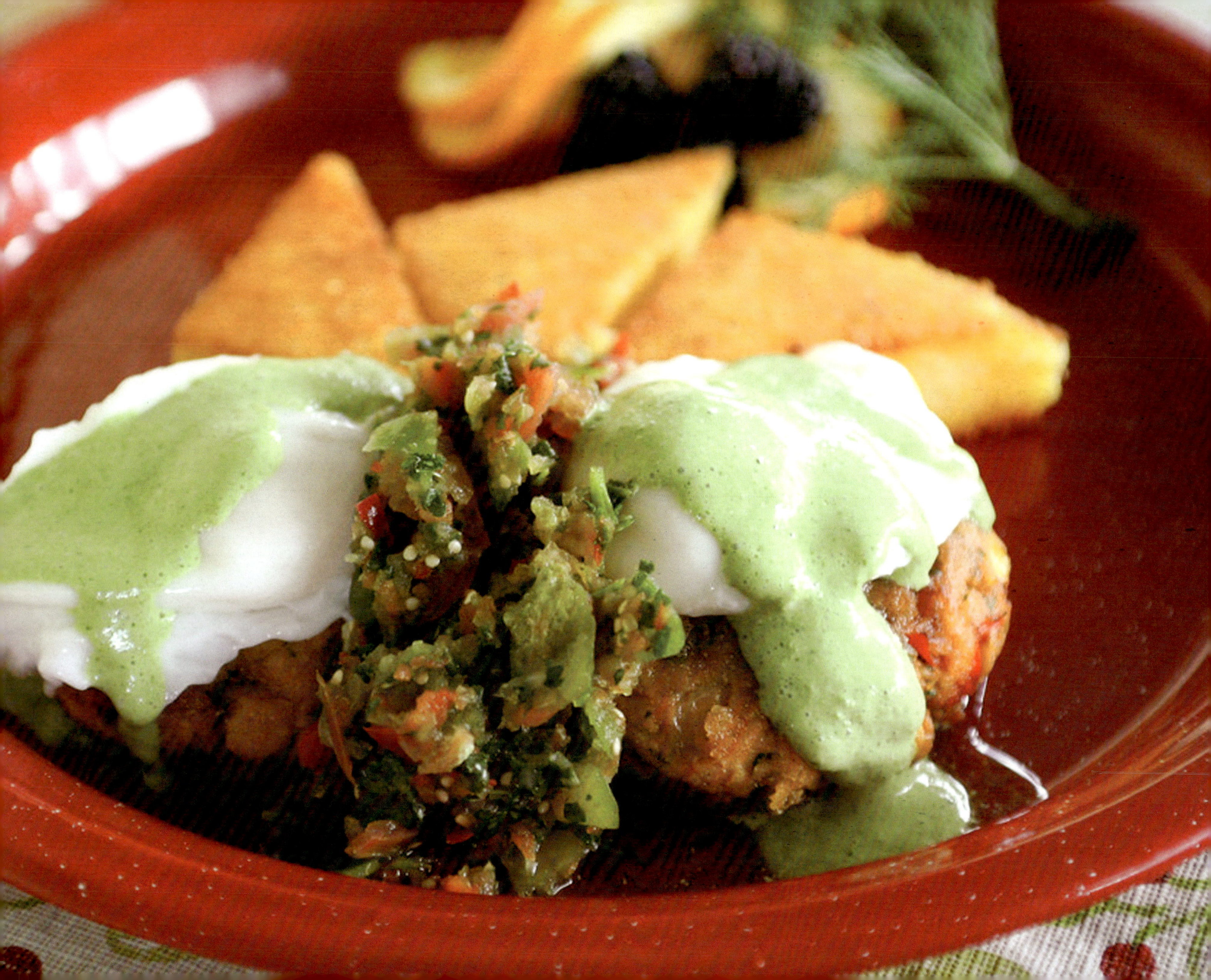

Masa Corn Cakes with Poached Eggs, Salsa Fresca and Cilantro Cream

These corn cakes are my rendition of the South American Arepa, corn cakes stuffed with a savory filling. The addition of fresh corn, onions, peppers, and spices gives these crunchy, moist cakes lots of flavor and texture. We pan sear the cakes in oil to make a nice crust and then finish them in the oven.

serves 4-6

Ingredients

- 1 yellow onion, finely diced
- 1 green pepper, finely diced
- 1 red pepper, finely diced
- 1 jalapeno pepper, seeds removed and minced
- 2 Tablespoons minced garlic
- 2 Tablespoons vegetable oil
- 1 ear of corn, shucked, kernels removed
- 3 bunches cilantro, coarsely chopped
- 1 Tablespoon chili powder
- 1 Tablespoon ground cumin
- 4 cups masa flour
- 4 cups hot water
- 3/4 stick melted butter
- Vegetable oil for cooking
- 8 to 12 eggs
- Salsa Fresca
- Cilantro Cream

1. In a large skillet, sauté the onion, peppers and garlic in vegetable oil until soft.

2. Add the corn, cilantro, chili powder and cumin, and cook for two minutes longer. Set aside.

3. Melt the butter and set aside.

4. In a large bowl, place the masa flour and make a well in the center. Add the hot water, melted butter, and the pepper mixture. Mix thoroughly and season well with salt and pepper. Let set for 15 minutes.

5. Using your hands, form 3-inch patties of the masa mixture. Place on a baking sheet lined with plastic wrap.

6. Bring a large skillet with water to simmer, for poaching the eggs.

7. In a nonstick pan, heat enough oil to cover the bottom of the pan. Add the masa cakes and when golden brown on one side, turn over and place the pan in 350 degree oven to finish cooking.

8. Drop the eggs in the poaching water, two per person, and cook to desired firmness.

9. Place two masa cakes on each serving plate, top each take with an egg, and garnish with the Salsa Fresca and Cilantro Cream (see recipes in The Finishing Touches section).

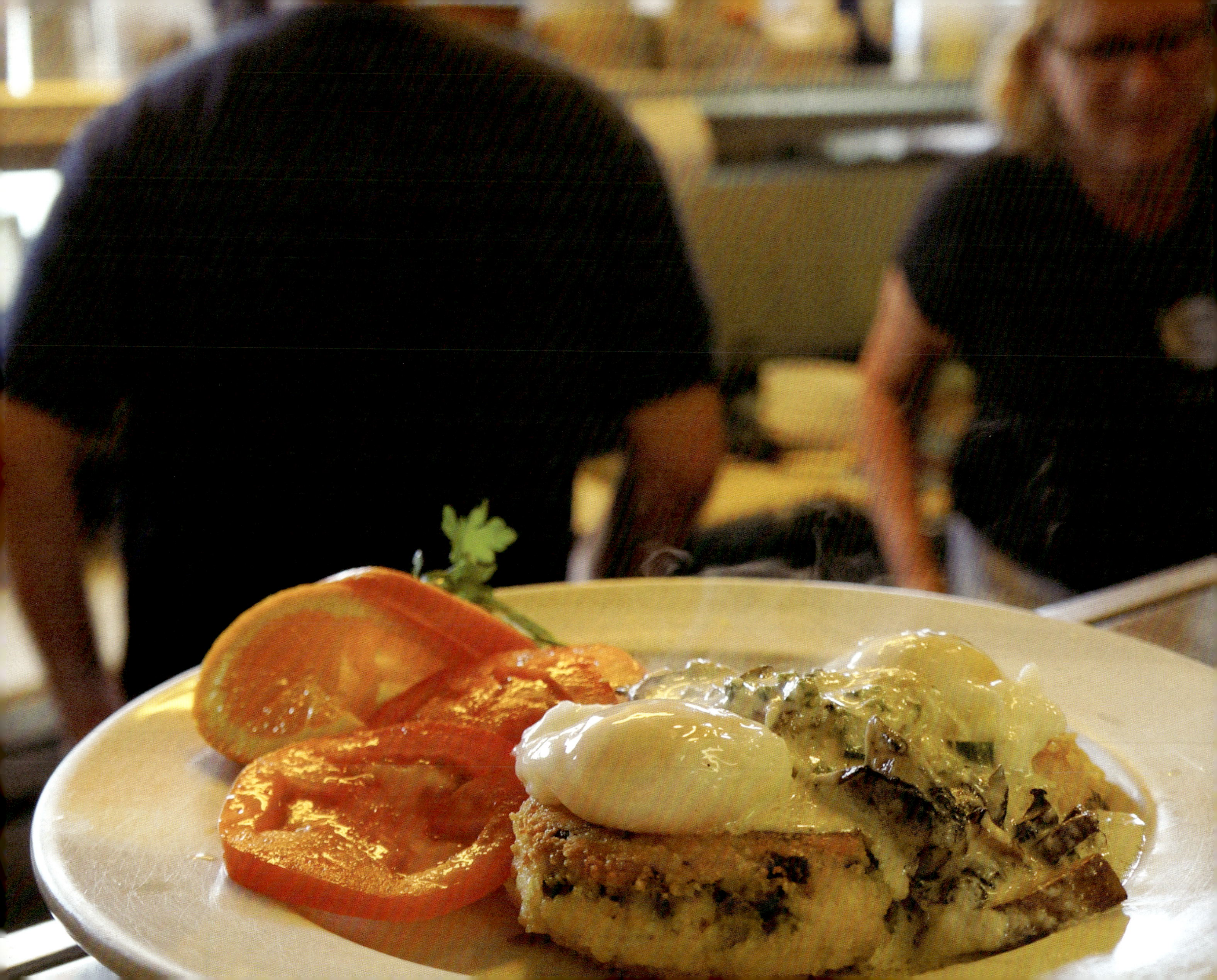

Crispy Risotto Kale Cakes with Poached Eggs and Gorgonzola Mushroom Cream Sauce

These cakes are wonderful for brunch! You can make the risotto mixture up to 3 days ahead. Store in the refrigerator, then form into cakes before cooking. (I purposely made these gluten-free for those with dietary restrictions, but you may certainly use regular Panko bread crumbs if you prefer.)

serves 6

Ingredients

- 1 quart half and half
- 2 cups vegetable broth
- 1 stick butter
- 2 Tablespoons olive oil
- 1/2 cup yellow onion, finely diced
- 1 cup fresh kale, finely chopped
- 2 Tablespoons minced garlic
- 2 1/4 cups Arborio rice
- 1 cup white wine
- 1 cup grated Parmesan
- 2 Tablespoons chopped parsley
- Salt and pepper
- 1 cup gluten-free bread crumbs (Panko brand)
- Vegetable or olive oil for browning the Risotto Cakes
- 1 dozen poached eggs

1. In a saucepan, heat the half and half and broth together and keep warm.

2. In a 4-quart or larger saucepan, melt the butter and olive oil; add the onions and cook on low heat, stirring until softened, about 5 minutes.

3. Add the kale and garlic and continue cooking until the kale is wilted.

4. Add the rice, stirring to coat the grains, and when the rice has turned a pale golden color, pour in the wine, stirring or whisking constantly until the wine is fully absorbed. With a ladle continue adding the hot mixture and stirring until all has been added and fully absorbed. The rice should be al dente (just slightly firm) by this point.

5. Stir in the Parmesan and parsley; season with salt and pepper to taste. Spread the mixture on to a cookie sheet cover lightly with saran wrap, and refrigerate.

6. When the mixture is cold, shape into small cakes and coat both sides with the bread crumbs. Keep refrigerated until ready to cook.

7. Pre-heat oven to 350 degrees. In a large skillet, heat some vegetable or olive oil and when hot, add your cakes. When they are crispy and golden brown on the bottom, turn the cakes over to crisp the second side.

Keep warm in oven while you prepare your sauce. When ready to serve, place two cakes along with two poached eggs on top and cover with sauce.

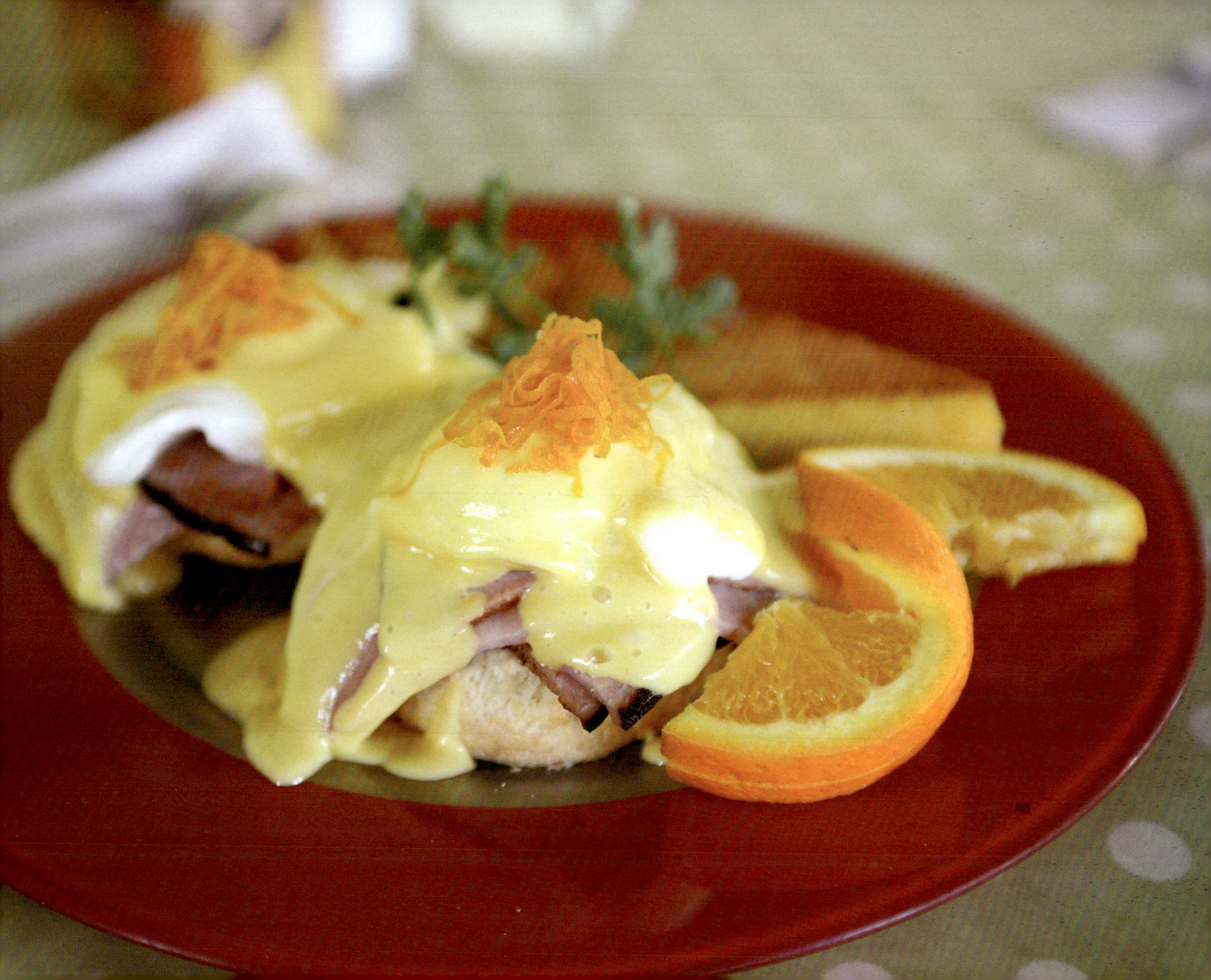

Christina (CC)

Eggs Benedict with Black Forest Ham on Orange Cream Biscuit with Orange Hollandaise Sauce

The orange biscuits are very delicate and they melt in your mouth.
This is a great Sunday brunch entrée. Just make sure to have Bloody Mary's or Mimosas to go with it!

serves 6

Ingredients

1 pound thinly sliced Black Forest ham
6 Orange Cream Biscuits
   (in Glorious Baked Goods section)
1 stick butter, melted
12 eggs for poaching
Orange Hollandaise Sauce (See recipe in Finishing Touches Section)

1. Split the biscuits and brush with melted butter; place on a baking sheet and toast in a 350 degree oven until golden brown.

2. Heat the ham slices in a skillet.

3. Poach and drain the eggs.

4. Layer biscuit, ham, and egg, and top with Hollandaise Sauce

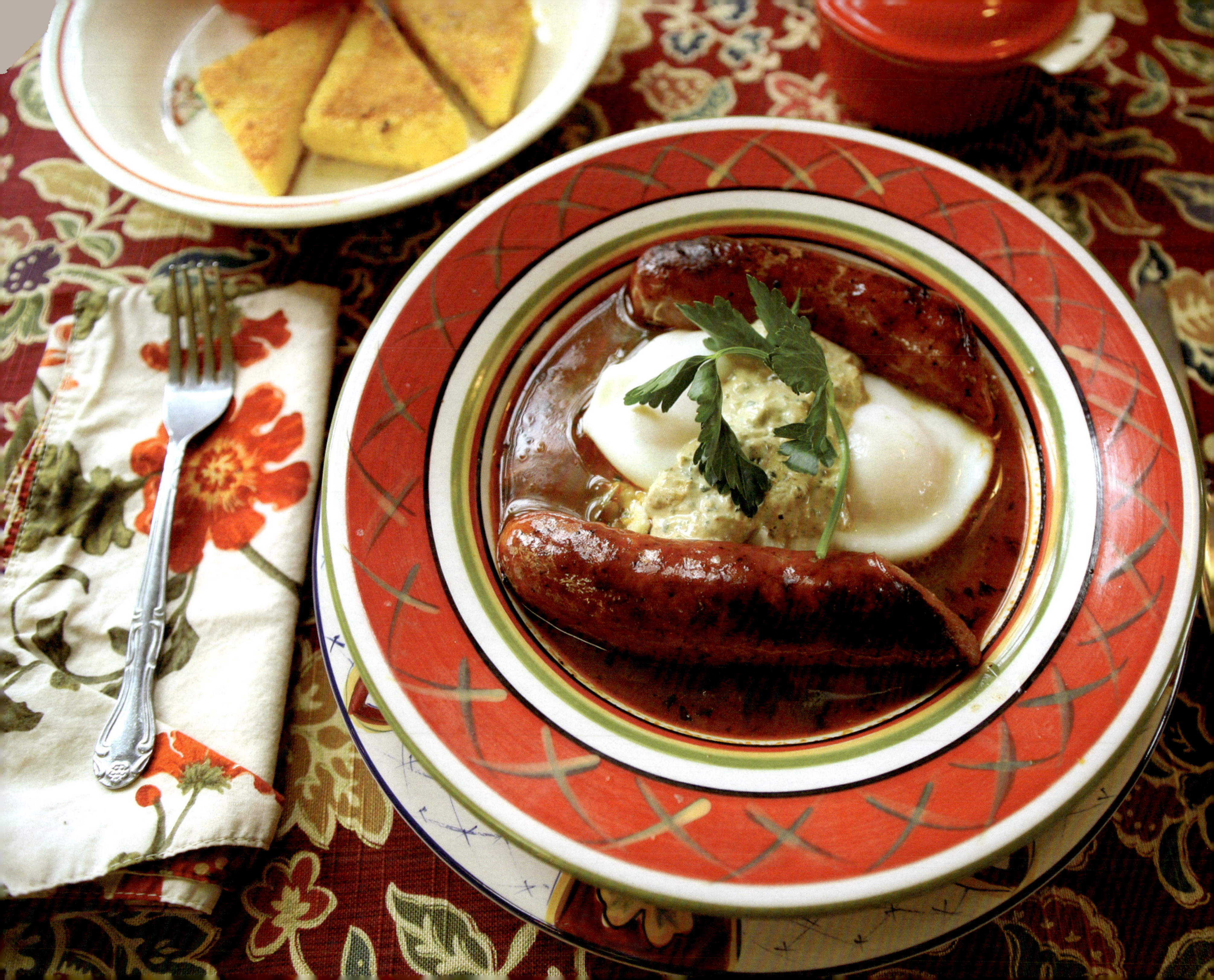

Eggs Creole with Linguisa Sausage, Cheddar Grits and Remoulade Sauce

Serves 6

Ingredients

12 eggs
6 Linguisa sausages

Creole Sauce

2 Tablespoons olive oil
1/2 small yellow onion, diced
1/2 red bell pepper, seeded and finely diced
1/2 green bell pepper, seeded and finely diced
1/2 cup diced tomato
2 Tablespoons minced garlic

1 teaspoon chili powder
1 teaspoon ground cumin
1 teaspoon paprika
4 cups chicken broth
1 Tablespoon chopped parsley

1. Heat olive oil in a heavy-bottomed pot; sauté peppers, tomato and onion until soft.

2. Stir in garlic and spices and sauté for 5 minutes. Add chicken broth and simmer, uncovered, for 30 minutes longer. Set aside and keep hot.

---

1. Cut sausages in half and sauté in a skillet until golden brown. Keep warm in oven.

2. Poach eggs to your liking.

3. Place a scoop of cheddar grits in the bottom of each serving bowl (See recipe in Finishing Touches), top with two poached eggs, and Creole Sauce.

Finish each serving with two pieces of sausage and a dollop of Remoulade Sauce (See recipe in Finishing Touches).

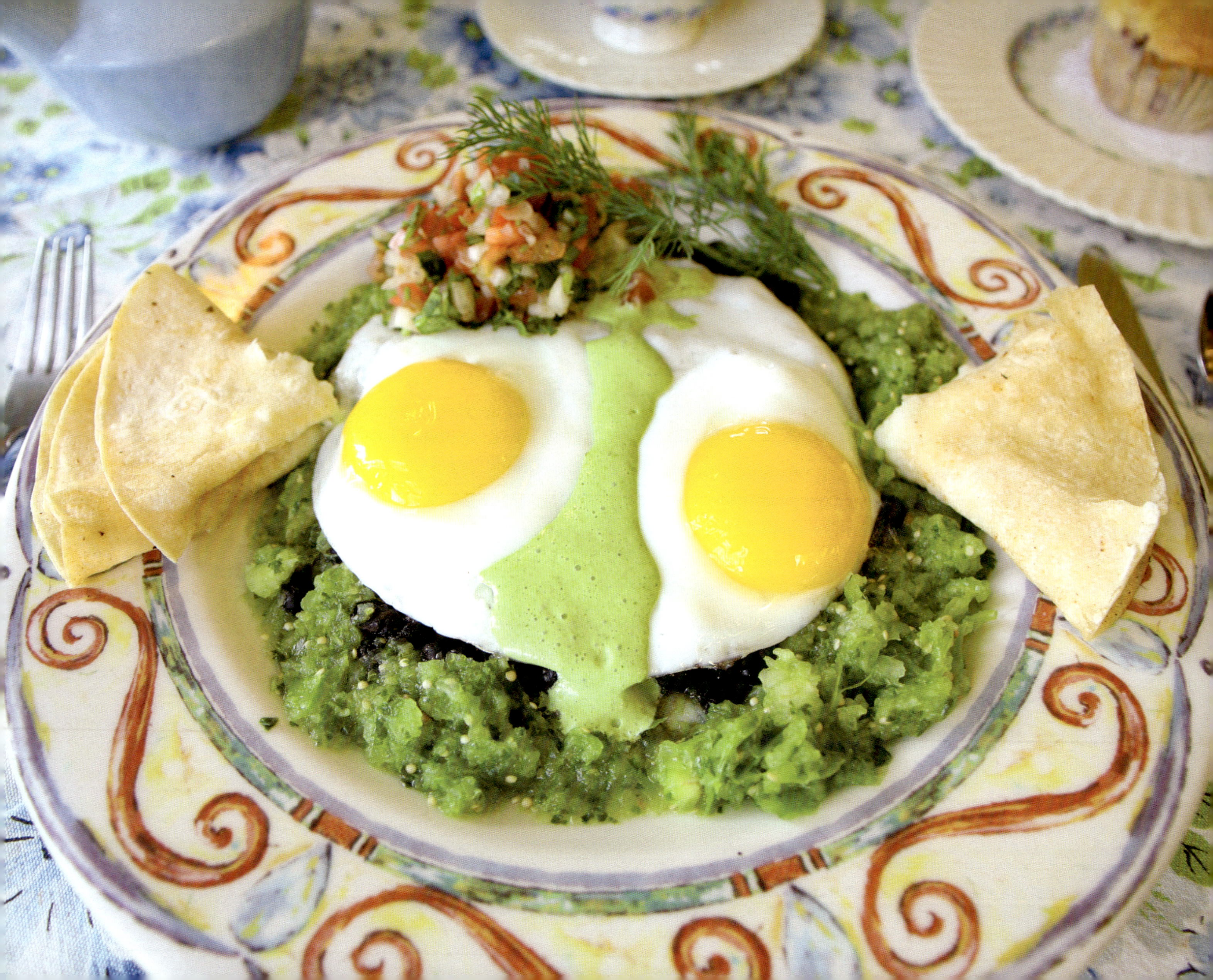

Huevos Rancheros with Black Beans, Tomatillo Sauce, Pepper Jack, Cilantro Cream & Smoked Salsa

serves 6

Ingredients

Tomatillo Sauce (see recipe in The Finishing Touches section)
2 dozen corn tortillas
1/2 pound Pepper Jack cheese, shredded
Smoked Salsa (See recipe in The Finishing Touches section)
Cilantro Cream (See recipe in The Finishing Touches section)

Black Beans:
2 Tablespoons oil
1 onion, finely diced
1 jalapeno pepper, seeded and minced
1 Tablespoon minced garlic
2 teaspoons ground cumin
2 teaspoons chili powder
1 teaspoon dried oregano leaves
2 bunches cilantro, chopped, including stems
6 cups water
1 Tablespoon salt
2 cups dried black beans, rinsed and picked over
12 eggs

For Beans:
1. In a skillet, heat oil and sauté the onion and jalapeno until soft.

2. Add the garlic and the spices; continue cooking for about two minutes.

3. Add the cilantro, 6 cups water and salt. Bring to a boil and add beans. Lower to a simmer and cook until beans are soft, about an hour and 15 minutes. Add more water as needed.

To Assemble:
1. Wrap the tortillas in foil and place in a preheated 350 degree oven to warm.

2. Heat the Tomatillo Sauce and black beans seperately.

3. Place 2 tortillas per person on ovenproof plates.
Cover with beans, two eggs (any style), Tomatillo Sauce, and Pepper Jack; place in the oven to melt the cheese.

4. Remove from oven and top with Smoked Salsa and Cilantro Cream. Serve extra tortillas on the side.

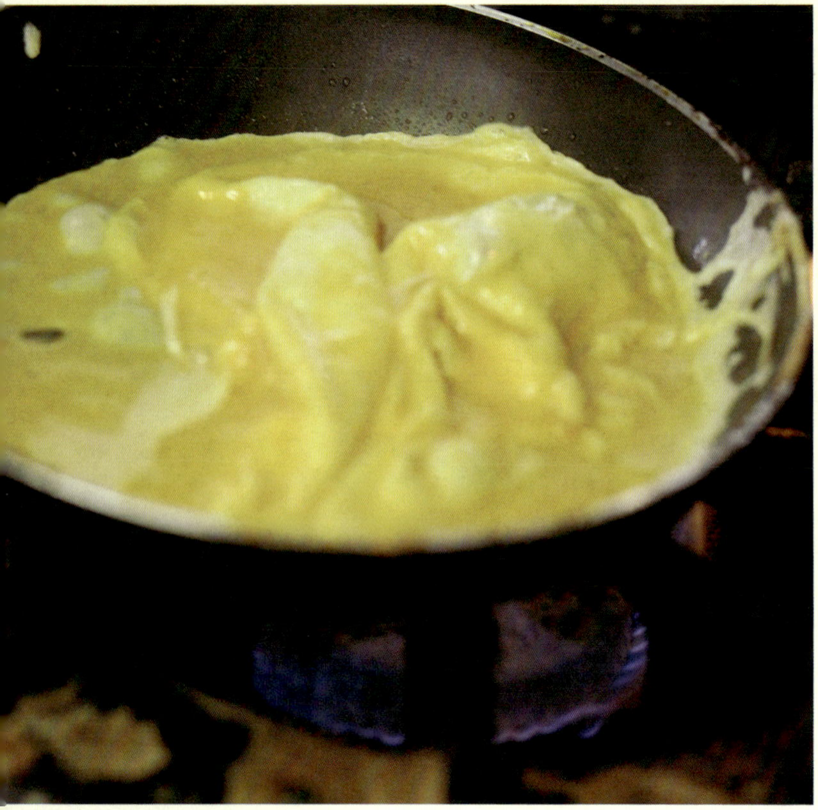
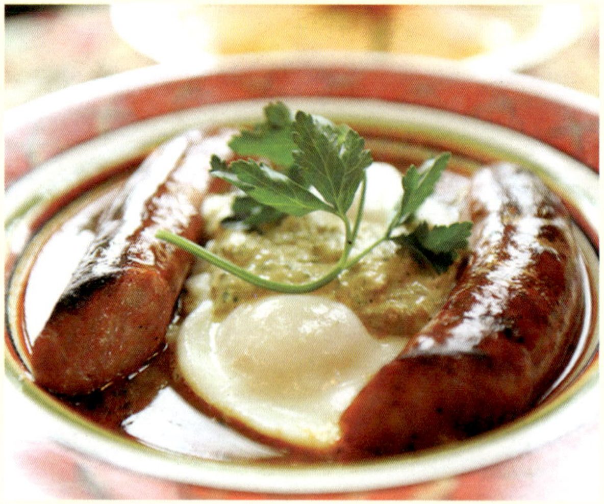
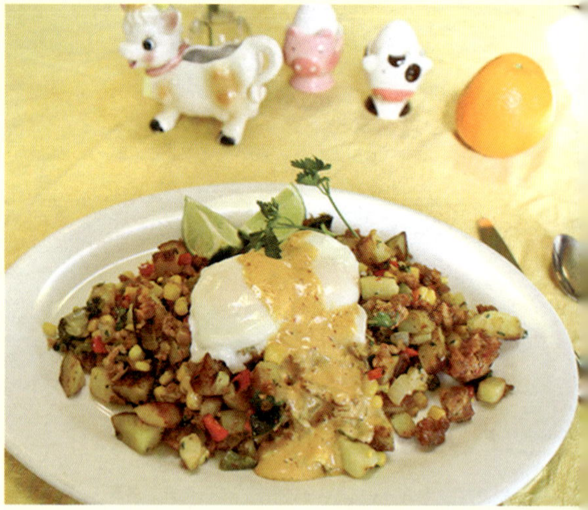
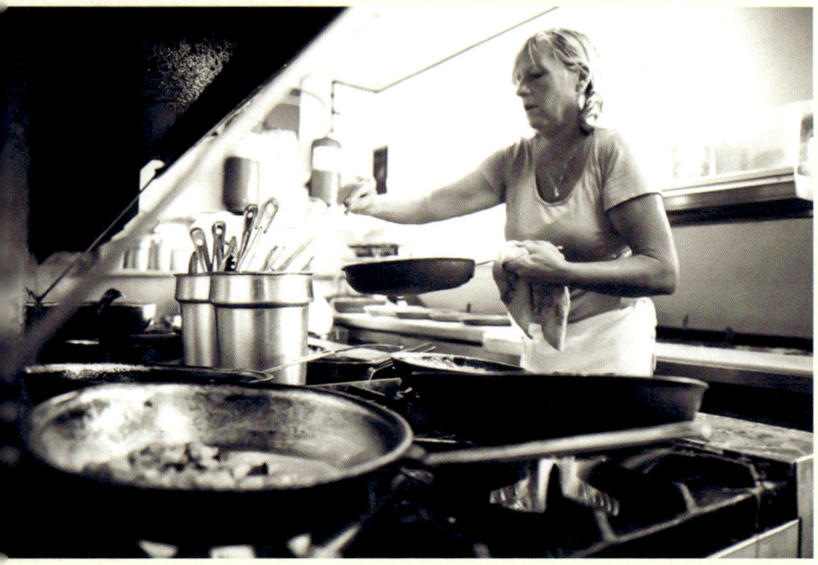
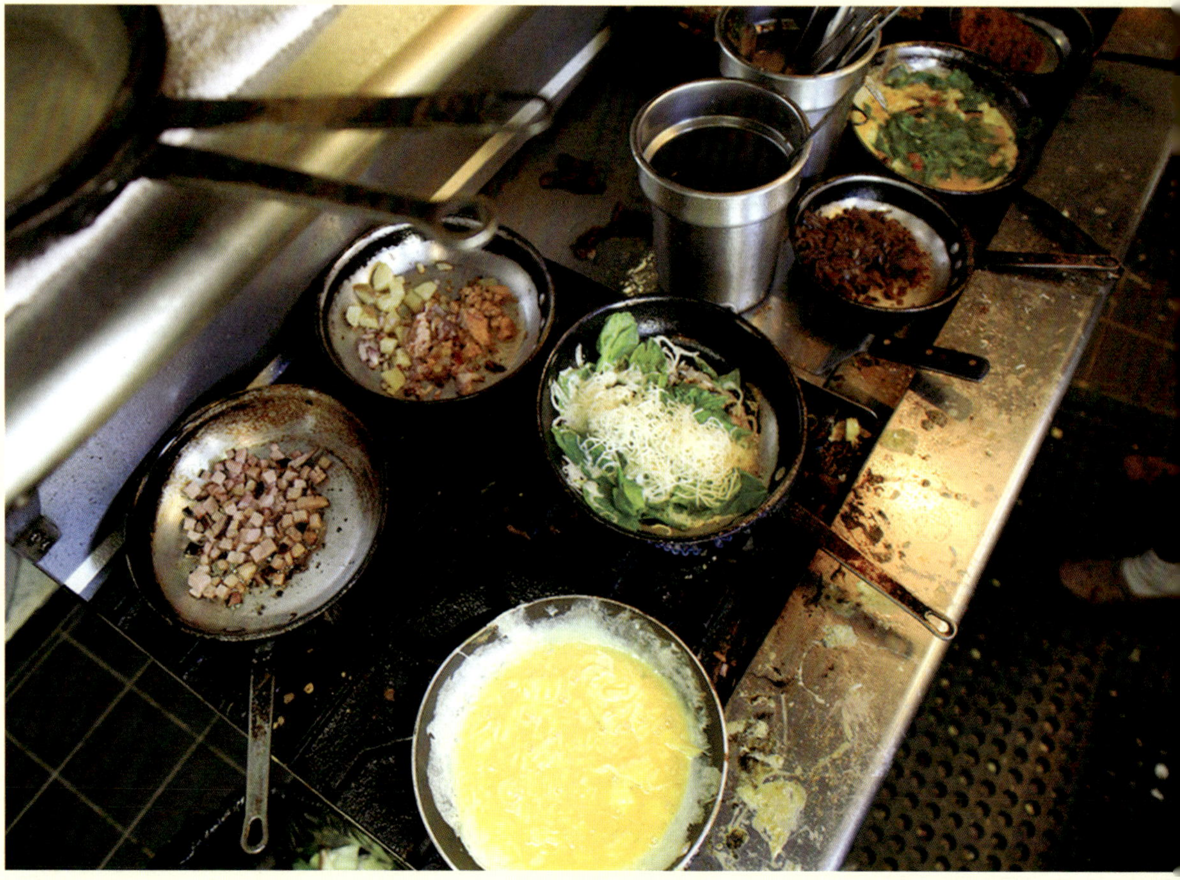

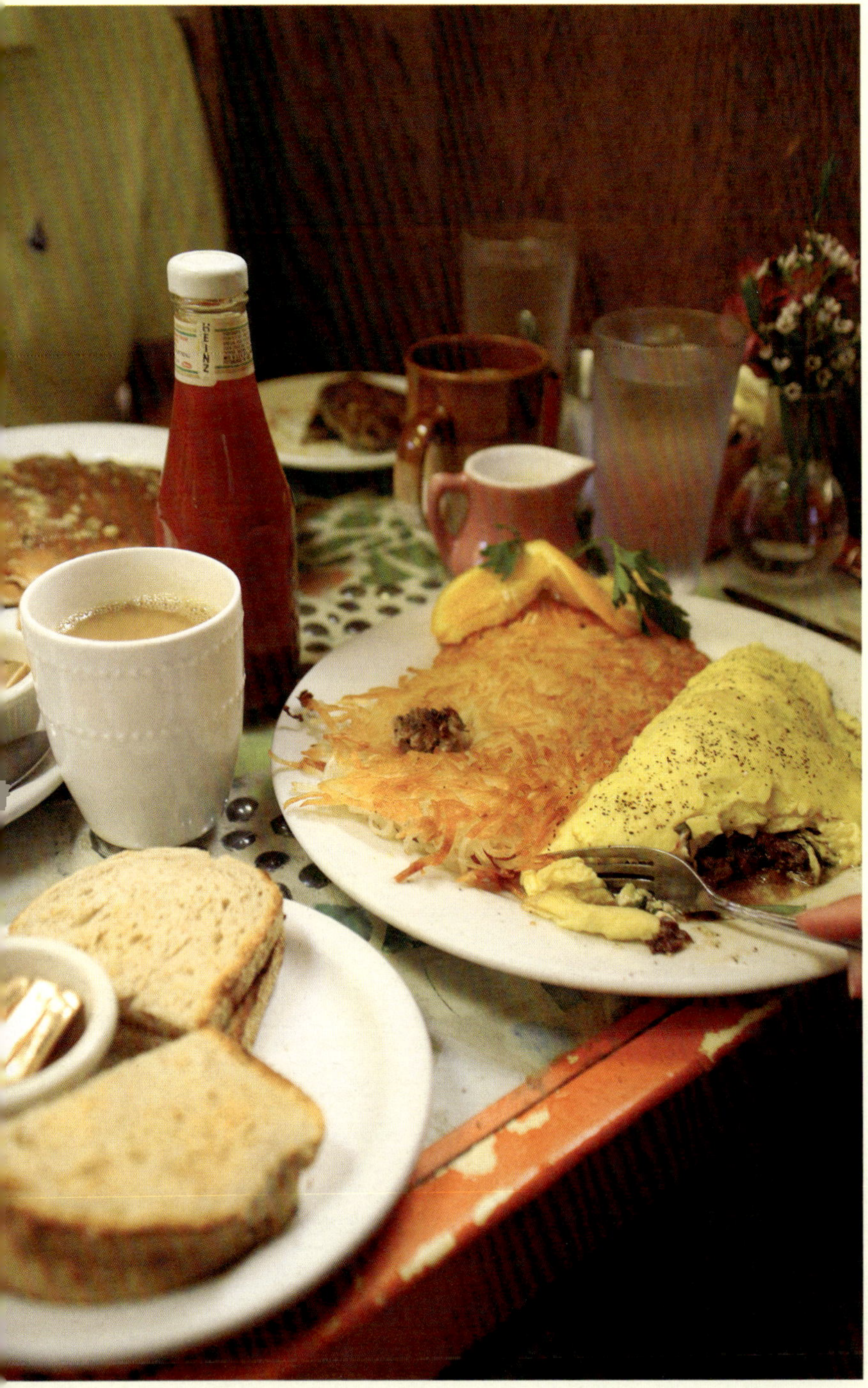

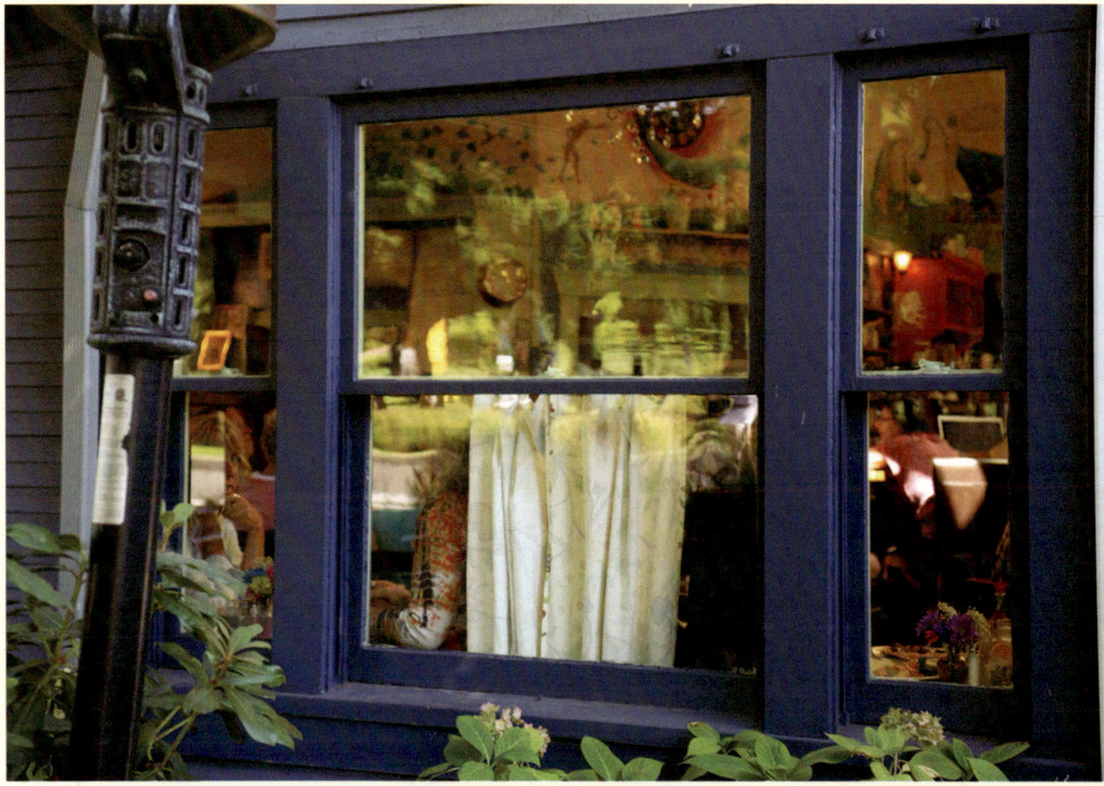

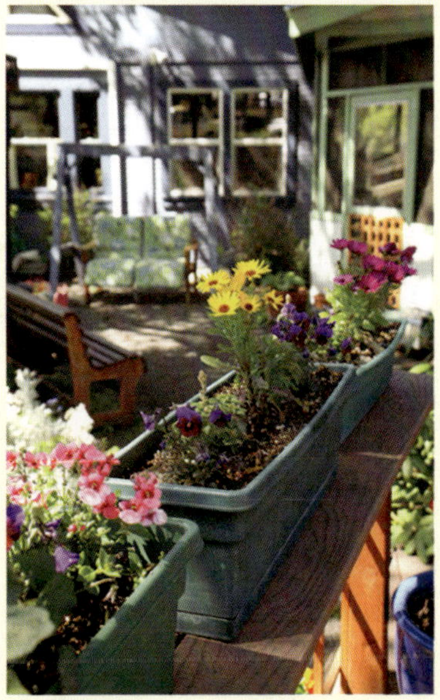

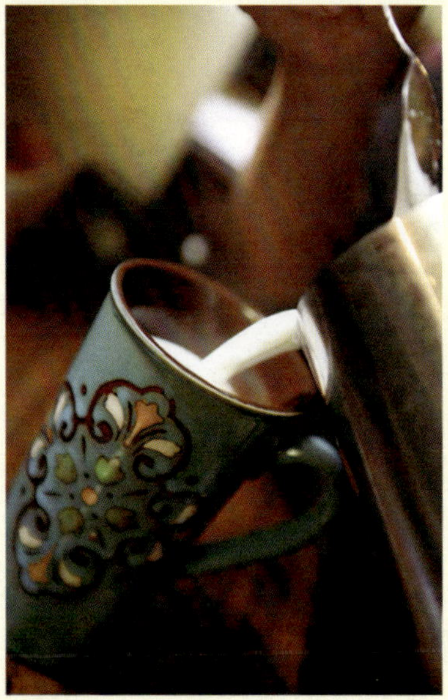

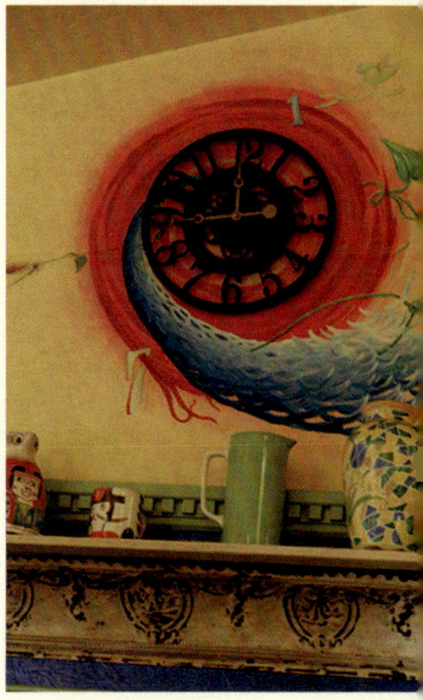

While cooking at Bridge Creek, Marion Cunningham (author of the revised *Fannie Farmer Cookbook*) came to me and said.. "Patty, can you teach me how to make an omelet? I have a cooking class tomorrow for a group of ladies and I don't know what to do!"

My first food photography for Chocolatier Magazine

(Bad 80's perm!)

Bridge Creek

I graduated from the CIA in 1986 and decided that I wanted to head back to the bay area. I landed a gig at Bridge Creek in Berkeley, as the kitchen manager, a recently opened breakfast restaurant on Shattuck Avenue. It was located two doors down from Chez Panisse, in an old Victorian.

Bridge Creek was challenging and stifling, but exciting because we were on the map. John Hudspeth, the owner, was good friends with Marion Cunningham (author of The "Revised" Fannie Farmer Cookbook and she was our menu consultant. We were the breakfast "IT" place and it was very exciting because of all the press that we were receiving. One of our specialty menu items was "Heavenly Hot's", which was comprised of sixteen delicate, silver dollar pancakes. They were featured in Chocolatier Magazine and many years later in the New York Times (see below).

Mimi Sheraton, in Time magazine, rated our very labor intensive Huevos Rancheros as "Meal of the Year" in 1986.

We served the best bacon ever (Nueske's out of Wisconsin) and it came in huge slabs that we had to hand slice. If I was lucky, I was allowed to go down to Chez Panisse, with a bacon slab in tow and used their slicer to slice the bacon. I remember feeling so jealous of the crew because they were having FUN and listening to LOUD music while they worked, things that were forbidden at Bridge Creek. I stayed at Bridge Creek for about a year and a half until I knew that it was time to move on. Bridge Creek shut it's doors soon after, but with each experience, you gain more and at the age of 27, I was ready for bigger things.

There were a few perks knowing John Hudspeth. One day, he pulled up to my apartment in Oakland in his bright red Cadillac convertible to take me to dinner at Chez Panisse. For those in the know, a private table was kept reserved, in the kitchen. To be able to observe the close workings of such an amazing chef (Paul Bertolli) and staff was a culinary highlight. I saved the handwritten menu from that night for over thirty years.

RECIPE REDUX: HEAVENLY HOTS, 1987
BY AMANDA HESSER

Sometimes the name of a dish is irresistible. Ratatouille. Financiers. Mooncakes. Oysters Rockefeller. Fallen soufflé. Anything confited. And my recent favorite, pudding chômeur, which translates to "unemployed-person pudding." (Biscuit dough baked in maple syrup and cream, it's a delight that Canadians have been keeping to themselves.)
Six years ago, when I began work on a cookbook of New York Times recipes, several readers wrote in about heavenly hots. There was no question: I had to try a recipe with that name.
Although heavenly hots sound like a late-night cable offering, they're nothing more salacious than pancakes. Once you make them, you'll understand the name. They are so feathery, creamy, tangy — so heavenly —

HEAVENLY HOTS

Have there ever been lighter, more delicate pancakes? Although divine with warm maple syrup and sweet butter, they would also be celestial with fresh fruit.

YIELD: Approximately 48 pancakes
DIFFICULTY:
PREPARATION: 10 minutes plus cooking time

2 cups sour cream
4 large eggs, lightly beaten
¼ cup cake flour
3 tablespoons granulated sugar
½ teaspoon baking soda
½ teaspoon salt
Butter, to taste
Maple syrup, to taste

1. Preheat the oven to 200°F.
2. In a large bowl, whisk together the sour cream, eggs, cake flour, sugar, baking soda and salt, until well mixed.
3. Over medium-high heat, heat a lightly greased griddle or large, heavy skillet until very hot. The griddle is ready when a small amount of water sprinkled onto the surface immediately turns into dancing droplets.
4. Drop the batter by tablespoons, 1 inch apart, onto the griddle. Cook the pancakes for 40 to 45 seconds, until bubbles are just beginning to appear on the surface of the pancakes. Carefully turn them over with a small metal spatula and continue cooking the pancakes for another 40 to 45 seconds, until the second side is lightly browned. Transfer the pancakes to a baking sheet. Place the baking sheet in the preheated warm oven to keep the cooked pancakes warm while preparing the rest of the pancakes in the same fashion. Serve the pancakes hot with a pat of butter and maple syrup on each serving.

BACK STORY: Provocatively yet aptly named, these sour cream pancakes were served at Bridge Creek Restaurant in Berkeley, Calif., in the late 1980s.

Tereza

Liz

Marty

Chip

Nora

Beverages

Beverages

"The Morning After"
Bloody Mary   120
Chipotle Bloody Mary   120
Glory-rita   121
Orange Cremesicle   122
Raspberry Mojito   123
Tequila Sunrise   124

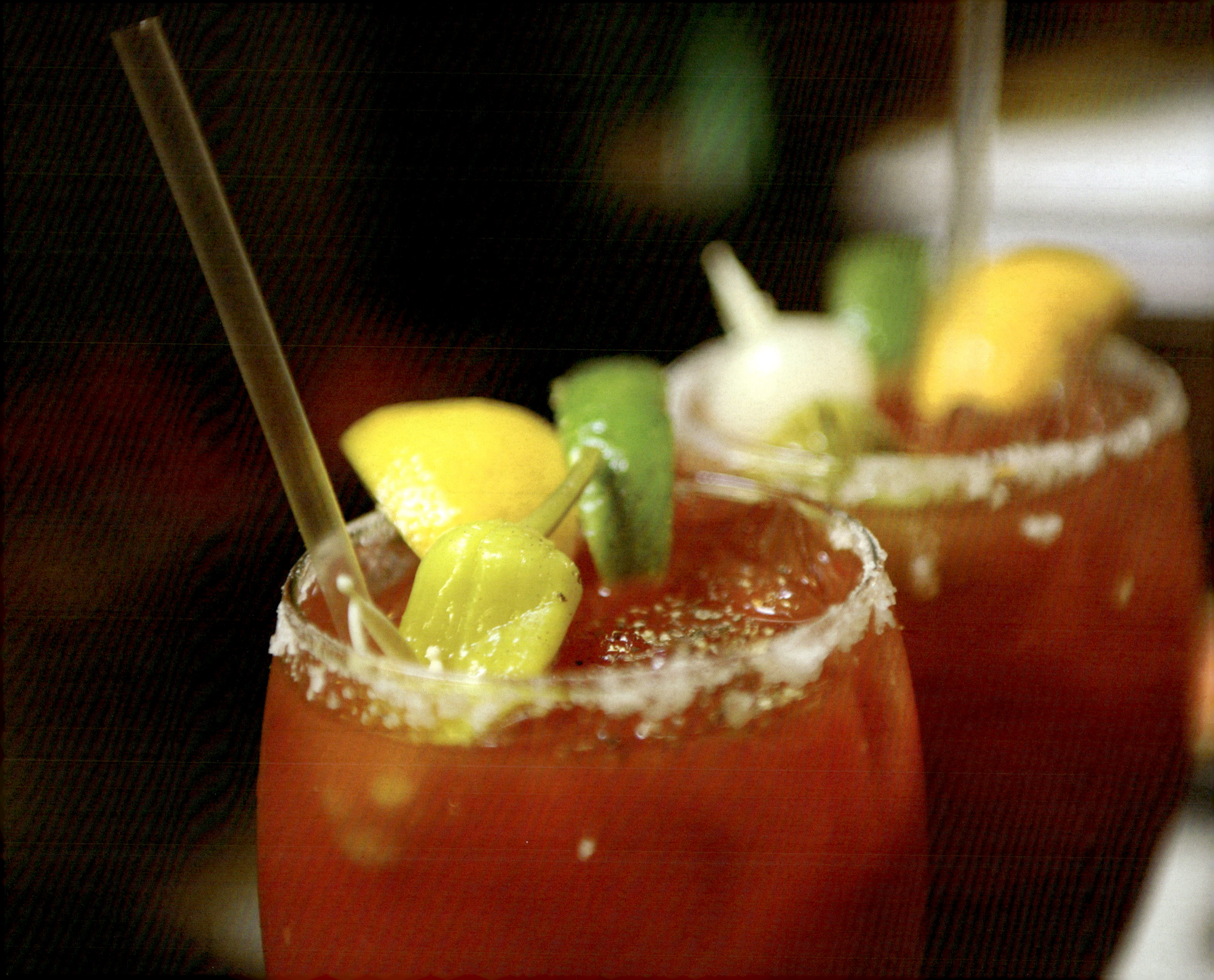

The 'Morning After' Bloody Mary

Great for Sunday brunch.
It is best to blend the mix the day before so flavors meld.

serves 6

Ingredients

Bloody Mary Mix:
1 (46 ounce) can tomato juice
1/2 cup bottled horseradish
2 Tablespoons green olive juice
1 Tablespoon Tabasco Sauce
1 Tablespoon Worcestershire Sauce
2 teaspoons cracked black pepper
1 teaspoon celery salt

For garnish:
6 cocktail swords
6 each: pimiento-stuffed olives, pickled cocktail onions, pepperoncini, lemon and lime wedge

For serving:
3 ounces, per serving, premium vodka
6 (16-ounce) glasses, chilled
1 cup kosher salt
1/2 cup lemon juice

1. In a blender, combine and blend the mix ingredients.

2. Prepare garnishes by spearing an olive, an onion, pepperoncini and lemon and lime wedges on each cocktail sword.

3. Place kosher salt and lemon juice in separate saucers; dip rims of the glasses into lemon juice and then into kosher salt.

4. Add ice, vodka and blended Bloody Mary mix.

Stir and insert the garnish.

Chipotle Bloody Mary

It is best to blend the mix the day before so flavors meld.

serves 6

Ingredients

Chipotle Bloody Mary Mix:
1 (46 ounce) can tomato juice
1/2 cup bottled horseradish
3 canned Chipotle Peppers in Adobo Sauce
1 Tablespoon Worcestershire
1 Tablespoon Chipotle Tabasco Sauce
Juice of one lemon or lime
2 teaspoons minced garlic
2 teaspoons cracked black pepper
1 teaspoon celery salt

For garnish:
6 cocktail swords
6 each: pimiento-stuffed olives, pickled cocktail onions pepperoncini, lemon and lime wedge

For serving:
3 ounces, per serving, premium vodka
6 (16-ounce) glasses, chilled
1 cup kosher salt
1/2 cup lemon juice

1. In a blender, combine and blend the mix ingredients.

2. Prepare garnishes by spearing an olive, an onion, pepperoncini and lemon and lime wedges on each cocktail sword.

3. Place kosher salt and lemon juice in separate saucers; dip rims of the glasses into lemon juice and then into kosher salt.

4. Add ice, vodka and blended Bloody Mary mix.

Stir and insert the garnish.

Glory-ita

This is Morning Glory's version of a margarita.

serves 1

Ingredients

2 ounces tequila
1 Tablespoon Grand Marnier
1 cup fresh-squeezed grapefruit juice

For serving:
1 cup kosher salt
1/2 cup grapefruit juice
Kosher salt
Lime wedge

1. Prepare margarita glass by placing 1/2 cup grapefruit juice and some Kosher salt in separate saucers. Dip rims in grapefruit juice and then in kosher salt to coat.

2. In a shaker, combine 1 cup grapefruit juice, tequila, Grand Marnier and a scoop of ice.

3. Shake and strain into the glass.

Garnish glass with lime wedge.

Orange Creamsicle

serves 1

Ingredients

3 ounces premium vodka
1 ounce Grand Marnier
1/2 cup fresh orange juice
1/2 cup half and half
Orange wedge to garnish

1. Combine ingredients in a shaker with ice.
2. Shake and pour over ice.
3. Garnish with an orange wedge.

Raspberry Mojito

Make the Mint Simple Syrup at least a day ahead and store in the refrigerator.

serves 1

Ingredients

Mint Simple Syrup:
4 bunches of fresh mint
2 cups sugar
2 cups water

For each cocktail:
1 cup fresh raspberries
Juice of one lime
3 to 6 fresh mint leaves
1 Tablespoon Mint Simple Syrup
2 shots light Bacardi Rum
Splash of club soda

To Garnish:
Lime slice and a sprig of mint

1. To make the syrup, combine mint bunches in a saucepan with sugar and water.

2. Simmer on low heat for 1/2 hour. Chill; strain out the mint.

3. To make a Mojito: muddle raspberries, lime juice, and fresh mint with the mint simple syrup in a cocktail shaker.

4. Add 2 shots of rum and ice. Shake and pour over ice. Finish with a splash of club soda.

Garnish with lime slice and a sprig of mint.

Tequila Sunrise

serves 1

Ingredients

1 cup fresh orange juice
3 ounces tequila
1/2 ounce Grenadine

To garnish:
Chilled, salted rimmed glass
Lime, strawberry and orange slice
with Maraschino cherries

Combine tequila and orange juice in a shaker with ice. Pour over ice. Top with 1/2 ounce Grenadine and garnish.

Relax.
Make yourself at home.

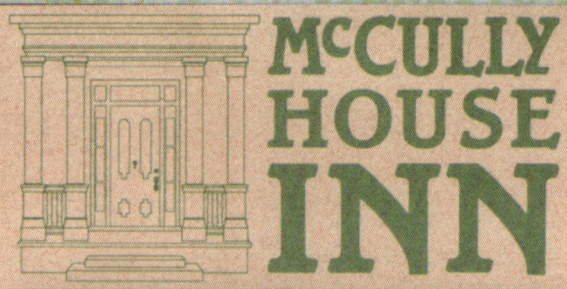

Tom Patty Phil

McCully House Inn
DINING & LODGING

FOR INFORMATION OR
RESERVATIONS CALL
(503) 899-1942

Patricia Groth and Phil Accetta, Proprietors

After leaving Bridge Creek, I headed back to San Francisco, for one final stint at 565 Clay, a hip restaurant located in the financial district. The year was 1987 and it was the same year that my father passed away from cancer at the age of 60. It was a devastating time for my family, as it happened very quickly.

It was during this time that a very good friend of mine, Janee Chandler, from my days in Allenspark and The Meadow Mountain Cafe, came to San Francisco with her new husband, Joe. They were headed to Oregon to check out some property that they had heard about in the Applegate Valley. I decided to tag along and we drove up together in my father's van. My friends loved the property and we were sitting in the van, in the Applegate, with their newly found real estate agent, Michael Donnelly, who I immediately felt a connection with. Janee and Joe were set on the property, and we were talking details when Janee perked up and said "Michael, now all you have to do is find Patty a restaurant!" and Michael replied "There is an inn for sale in Jacksonville, why don't you check it out on your way home?" We were headed back to San Francisco at that moment, and thought "what the heck?" We pulled up to this gorgeous white, classical 1860 mansion. We didn't even go beyond the front dining room and I knew that this was it, my restaurant, bigger than anything I could have ever imagined. We had some tea, got back in the van and drove straight to my mother's home. I had a sales pitch to deliver!

Apparently I was convincing, because my mother and I drove up to Oregon the following weekend (in the worst snow storm ever) and a deal was made, with Michael as my agent.

This was a huge undertaking not only was I going to open a restaurant, but I had an inn to run as well. Phil Accetta and I were in the same class at the CIA, and had been carrying on a long distance relationship since we had graduated. I knew that I was going to need help, so as crazy as it was, I called him up and asked him if he would like to open a restaurant with me. The answer was yes.

Within six months, Phil and I opened the doors of the McCully House Inn, along with Phil's childhood friend, Tom Weatherall. We arrived knowing nothing about the area and what it had to offer. I have to give many thanks to my friend Jerry Evans from the Jacksonville Inn (at that time was one the top 100 grossing restaurants in the country), in Jacksonville. He took us under his wing and helped us find purveyors, distributors, etc. and we were competition, right across the street!

We slowly took the Rogue Valley by storm. We were young, educated, inspired and fresh. The valley was excited, no one was doing anything innovative at that time, except for us and I loved running the Inn.

We had an 80 seat restaurant and three guest rooms, who saw the likes of John Travolta, Tom Cruise, Kirsty Ally and Parker Stevenson, and the best one of all Gerry Spence, the attorney famous for the OJ trials and Randy Weaver case. Five years into our venture, Phil and I discover that I am pregnant and that Phil no longer wishes to continue, as my partner in the inn. I had decisions to make and it meant giving up the inn. How could I possibly run this place by myself with a new born baby? I was thirty four by now and so excited to be a new mother, while not really understanding the impact that this decision would have on me. I had been working 18 hours a day for five years straight and at that point I just wanted to be a mom to my new son, Adrian. We sold the inn and moved to Ashland and within six months I was so distraught over giving up the McCully House. All I had ever done my whole life was work, and I was now faced with a baby that I adored, but with no identity and no income.

Phil and I stayed together as a couple for another year and then parted ways when Adrian was a year and a half. Although we didn't continue as a couple, we did remain a family and Phil was so supportive of my later endeavor, Morning Glory. He would come to my house every morning at 3:45, to take care of Adrian, so that I could go to work!

The Finishing Touches
Butters, Chutneys, Salsas, Sauces, Syrups and Others

The Finishing Touches
Butters, Salsas, Chutneys, Sauces, Syrups and Others

Butters 132
Walnut Butter
Lemon Butter
Hazelnut Amaretto Butter

Salsas 134
Salsa Fresca
Smoked Tomatillo Salsa
Cilantro Cream

Chutneys
Smoked Tomato Chutney 135
Sun-dried Cherry
   Cranberry Chutney 136

Sauces
Fresh Horseradish Cream 137
Tomatillo Sauce 138
Basil Pesto 139
Remoulade Sauce 140
Mushroom Gorgonzola Cream Sauce 141
Orange Chipotle Hollandaise 142
Chipotle Lime Hollandaise 142
Orange Hollandaise 142

Syrups 144
Marionberry Syrup
Mango Syrup
Raspberry Syrup
Dark Cherry Syrup

Others
Caramelized Onion 145
Apple Compote 146
Crispy White Cheddar Polenta 148
Cheddar Grits 148

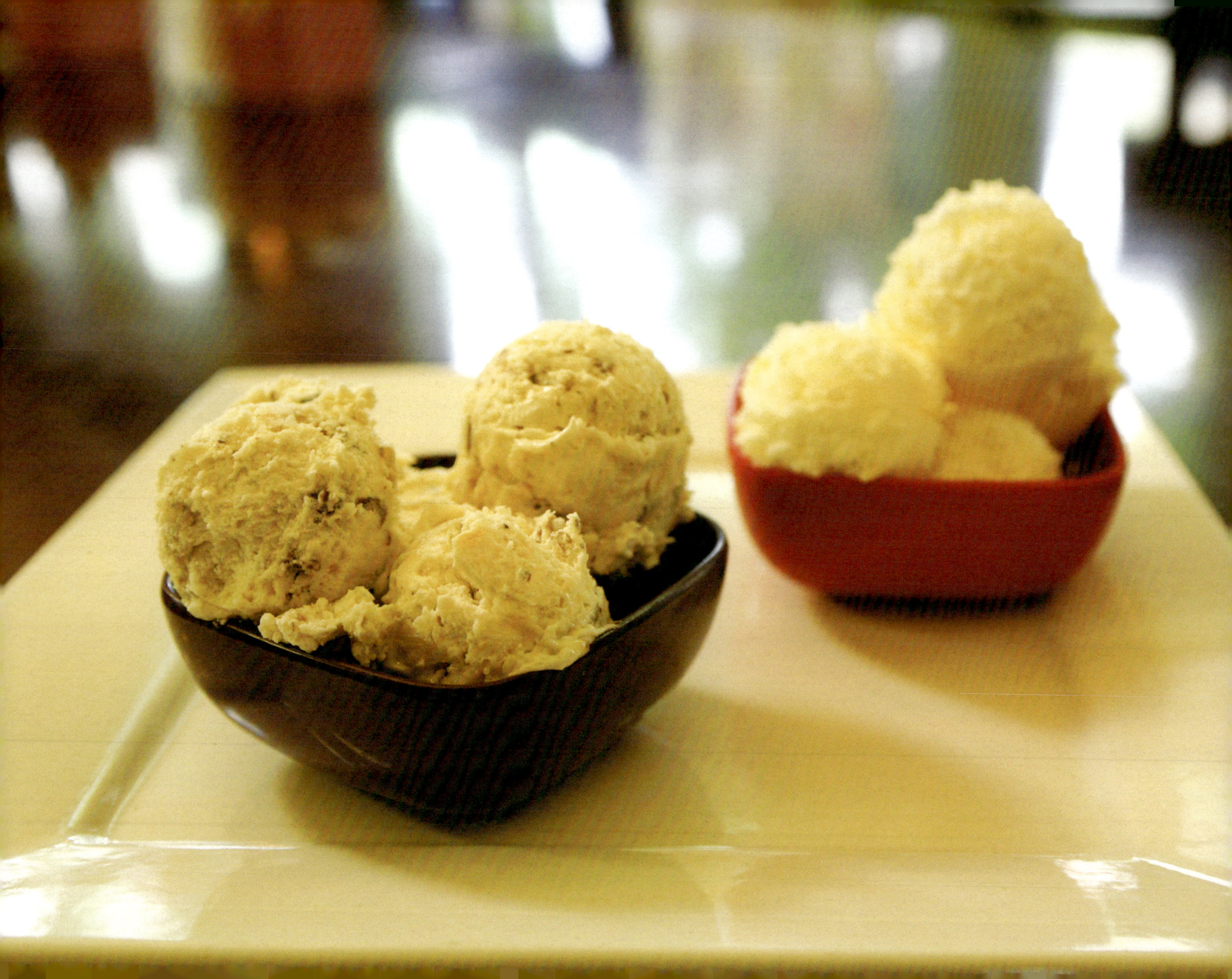

Walnut Butter

We serve this flavorful butter with our Oatmeal Pancakes and various other creations such as waffles, French toast and our berry muffins. It keeps beautifully in the refrigerator.

makes 3 cups

Ingredients

1 pound salted butter, softened
1 cup brown sugar
1 cup white sugar
2 cups walnut pieces
1 teaspoon walnut extract

1. Toast walnuts on a baking sheet in a 325 degree oven until golden brown. Approximately 10 minutes. Cool.

2. With an electric mixer, cream the butter and sugar until soft and fluffy.

3. Beat in the extract and nuts.

Refrigerate in a sealed container. When chilled, it is ready to use.

Lemon Butter

This butter, inspired by a recipe from my stint at the Campton Place Hotel in San Francisco, is wonderful on pancakes, waffles, and French toast. It is a longtime staple on our menu, and loved by all!

makes 3 cups

Ingredients

For reduction:
3 to 6 lemons, depending on juiciness
1 cup lemon juice
1 cup white sugar

For butter:
1 pound salted butter, softened
1/2 cup white sugar

1. Start by zesting 3 lemons.

2. Set aside zest.

3. Juice the lemons to make 1 cup juice.

4. Combine 1 cup lemon juice and 1 cup sugar then reduce until syrupy. Set aside to cool to room temperature..

5. With an electric mixer, whip the butter until creamy.

6. Slowly drip in syrup and mix until well combined. Add zest and refrigerate.

Amaretto Hazelnut Butter

makes 2 cups

Ingredients

2 sticks butter, softened
1 cup brown sugar
1/2 cup sugar
1 cup hazelnuts, toasted, skinned, chopped
1/2 cup Amaretto

1. In kitchen aid, add softened butter and sugars and beat for 5 minutes to dissolve sugars.

2. Add the nuts.

3. Turn the speed to low and slowly drizzle in the Amaretto. Chill.

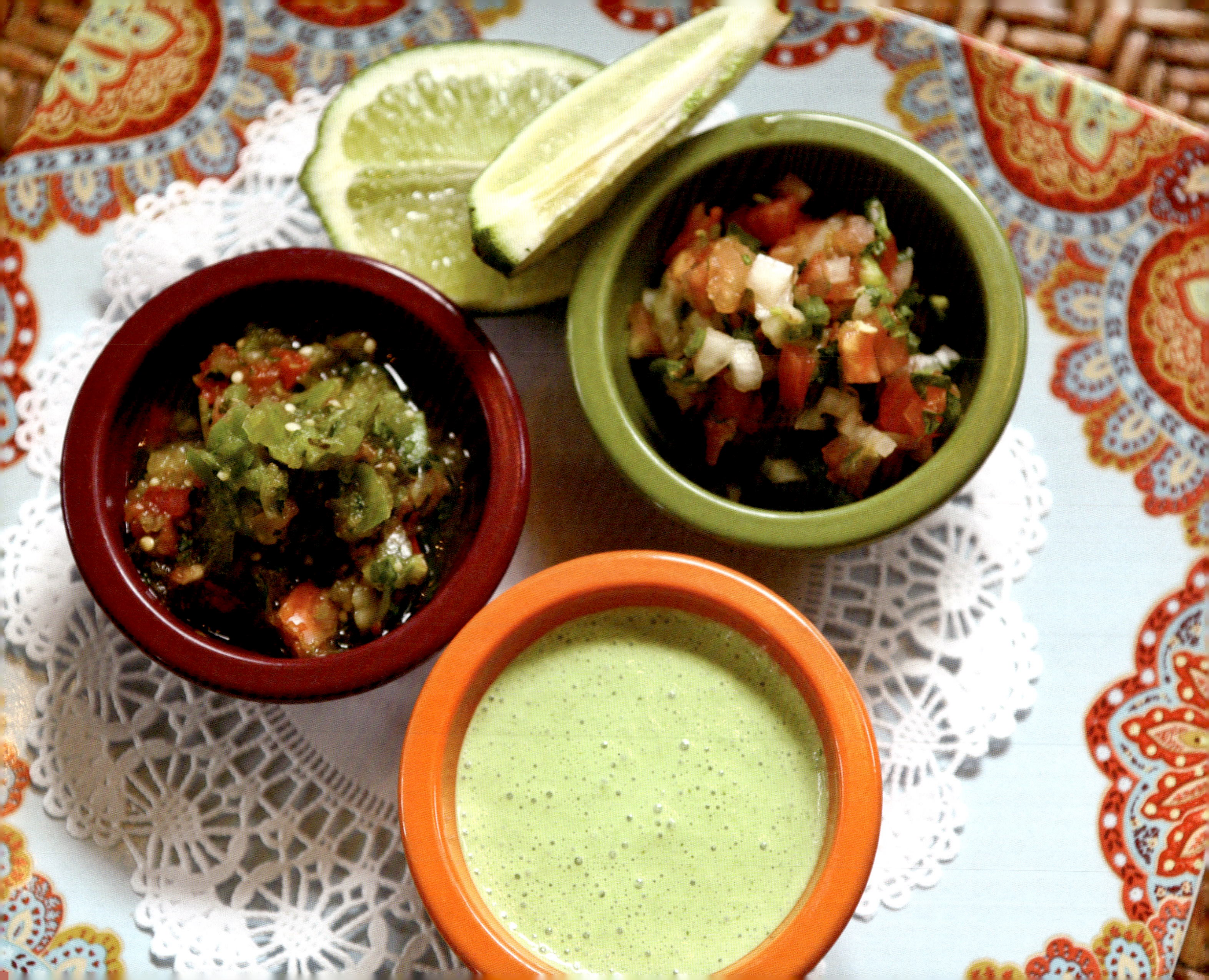

Smoked Tomatillo Salsa

This salsa is spectacular on Huevos Rancheros, in tacos or burritos, or simply with fresh tortilla chips and guacamole. It takes extra time because of the smoking, but the flavor is well worth the effort! Keeps well in the refrigerator.

for 1 quart

Ingredients

For the smoker:
1 yellow onion, skinned
1 red pepper, cored and seeded
1 green pepper, cored and seeded
3 tomatoes
8 tomatillos, husks removed
3 jalapenos
4 cloves whole garlic
Lemon juice and olive oil to moisten
Salt and pepper, to taste

To finish:
1 bunch chopped, fresh cilantro
Juice of one lemon
1 Tablespoon sugar
Salt and pepper, to taste

1. In a large bowl combine smoker ingredients with lemon juice and olive oil to moisten.

2. Place ingredients on a rack in a hot smoker, and smoke until golden brown. Remove and chill.

3. To finish the salsa, puree in a food processor. Stir in chopped cilantro, the lemon juice and sugar. Season with salt and pepper to taste. Chill and serve!

Salsa Fresca

This salsa is a staple at Morning Glory. We use it on Huevos Rancheros, Breakfast Burritos, and Masa Corn Cakes with Poached Eggs. Best when made the day of serving.

makes 1 1/2 cups

Ingredients

2 ripe tomatoes or a mix of sweet pear and golden tomatoes, finely diced
1/2 minced yellow onion
1 to 2 jalapenos, seeds removed and minced
1 Tablespoon minced garlic
1 Tablespoon chopped, fresh cilantro
1 Tablespoon vegetable oil
Juice of 1 to 2 limes, strained, to taste
Salt and pepper to taste

Combine all ingredients. Season well with salt and pepper.

Cilantro Cream

makes 1 1/2 cups

Ingredients

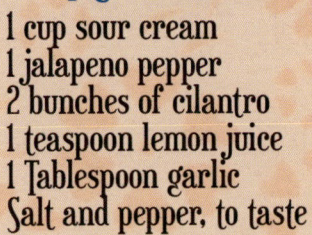

1 cup sour cream
1 jalapeno pepper
2 bunches of cilantro
1 teaspoon lemon juice
1 Tablespoon garlic
Salt and pepper, to taste

Combine in a blender and puree. Chill until needed.

Smoked Tomato Chutney

Ingredients

10 garden fresh, medium-sized tomatoes, organic is best!
1 red onion, small diced
1 Tablespoon minced fresh ginger
1/4 cup currants
1 1/2 cups red wine vinegar
1 cup sugar
Salt and pepper, to taste

1. Core the tomatoes, place on a smoking grate and put in hot smoker and smoke until the skin is golden brown.

2. Pull from the smoker and cool. Peel off the skin, any little bits left on is fine.

3. Small dice the tomatoes, reserving any liquid.

4. In a heavy-bottomed stainless steel pot, saute the onions along with the ginger, until soft.

5. Add the tomatoes, currants, red wine vinegar and sugar.

6. Bring to a boil, lower the heat and simmer for 1- 1 1/2 hours, stirring frequently.

Sun-Dried Cherry Cranberry Chutney

This cherry chutney is served with our Tandoori Tofu dish. Great either hot or cold and keeps well in the refrigerator.

makes 3 cups

Ingredients

1/2 red onion, small diced
2 (14 ounce) cans whole cranberry sauce or
2 (14 ounce) bags fresh cranberries
1 cup sun-dried cherries
1 cup sugar
1/2 cup red wine vinegar
1/2 cup cranberry juice
Salt and Pepper, to taste

1. In a heavy-bottomed stainless steel pot, saute the red onion in some butter and olive oil. Add rest of ingredients and bring to a simmer until thick, about 20 minutes.

Add salt and pepper to taste.

Fresh Horseradish Cream

makes 1 cup

Ingredients

1 cup sour cream
2 Tablespoons chopped fresh horseradish
2 Tablespoons chopped scallions
1 Tablespoon chopped parsley
2 teaspoons Dijon mustard
Salt and pepper, to taste

1. Peel a chunk of horseradish and add to food processor. Chop as fine as possible.

2. In a bowl combine all of the ingredients. Refrigerate.

Tomatillo Sauce

This Sauce is used for our Huevos Rancheros and Breakfast Burrito, which are very popular. The effort is well worth it.
Tomatillos are a species of ground cherry, native to Mexico and widely naturalized in eastern North America.
They are yellow to light green in color, are covered in a papery husk and are quite sticky.

makes 2 quarts

Ingredients

2 pounds of tomatillos, husked and diced
1 yellow onion, small diced
1 bunch cilantro, chopped
2 Tablespoons garlic, minced
1 jalapeno pepper, minced
1 large can chicken broth or
2 quarts homemade chicken stock
1 Tablespoon cumin
1 Tablespoon chili powder
2 limes, juiced
1/2 cups olive oil
1 Tablespoon sugar
Salt and pepper, to taste

1. In a large stock pot, saute the tomatillos, garlic, cilantro, onion and jalapeno for 5 minutes.

2. Add the spices. Continue cooking for 2 minutes and then add the chicken broth.

3. Add the lime juice, sugar and salt and pepper. Simmer for 20 minutes.

4. Chill and then pureé in a blender until smooth.

Basil Pesto

makes 1 cup

Ingredients

1 cup packed fresh basil leaves
1/2 cup grated Parmesan
1/2 cup walnuts pieces
1/4 cup minced garlic
1 to 1 1/2 cups olive oil, depending on desired thickness
Salt and pepper, to taste

1. In a food processor, combine fresh basil, Parmesan, walnuts, and garlic.

2. With the machine running slowly, drip in olive oil. (To make either thicker or thinner, add more or less olive oil.)

Season with salt and pepper to taste.

Remoulade Sauce

serves 6

Ingredients

1 cup sour cream
1/2 yellow onion
1/2 tomato, cored
1 jalapeno pepper, seeded
1/2 bunch cilantro
2 garlic cloves
1/2 teaspoon chili powder
1/2 teaspoon ground cumin

Combine all ingredients in a blender or food processor; puree until smooth.

May be served hot or cold.

Mushroom Gorgonzola Cream Sauce

makes 3 Cups

Ingredients

2 Tablespoons olive oil
1 cup thinly sliced mushrooms
4 cups half and half
2 cups crumbled Gorgonzola cheese
2 Tablespoons scallions, thinly sliced

1. In a small saucepan, heat the olive oil and add the mushrooms. Cook until soft stirring frequently.

2. Stir in the half and half, Gorgonzola and scallions and cook until thickened, about 4 to 5 minutes.

Chipotle Lime Hollandaise Sauce

makes 2 cups

Ingredients

1 pound butter
4 egg yolks
4 limes, juiced
2 Tablespoons hot water
1 teaspoon Dijon mustard
Dash of Chipotle Tabasco
1 or 2 canned Chipotle Peppers in Adobo Sauce
Salt and pepper, to taste

1. In an electric blender, combine the yolks, lime juice, mustard, Chipotle Tabasco and hot water.

2. Melt the butter in a saucepan. With the blender running at medium speed, pour in the melted butter in a slow, steady stream. If sauce gets too thick, blend in a little more hot water.

Taste for seasoning and serve immediately.

Orange Hollandaise Sauce

makes 2 cups

Ingredients

1 pound butter
1/2 cup orange juice concentrate
6 egg yolks
3 Tablespoons hot water
1 Tablespoon lemon juice
1 teaspoon Dijon mustard
Dash of Tabasco
Zest of one orange, finely chopped
Salt and pepper, to taste

1. Melt the butter and keep it hot.

2. Simmer the orange juice concentrate in a small saucepan for 3 minutes to thicken.

3. In a blender: combine yolks, orange juice concentrate, hot water, lemon juice, mustard and Tabasco.

4. With motor running on slow speed, pour in the hot, melted butter in a slow, steady stream. (If the sauce becomes too thick, thin with more hot water.)

Season with orange zest, salt and pepper to taste. Set aside in a warm spot.

Orange Chipotle Hollandaise Sauce

makes 2 cups

Ingredients

1 pound butter
6 egg yolks
1/2 cup orange juice concentrate
1 Tablespoon Dijon mustard
1 Tablespoon lemon juice
2 Chipotle Peppers in Adobe Sauce
1 teaspoon Worchestersire sauce
1 teaspoon Chipotle Tabasco
Salt and pepper, to taste

1. In a blender, combine the yolks, Dijon, lemon juice, Chipotle Peppers, Tabasco and Worchestershire sauce.

2. Melt the butter and heat up the orange juice concentrate.

3. With the blender running, add warm orange juice concentrate and slowly drip in the melted butter.

If it's too thick, add more orange juice to thin it. Season with salt and pepper and serve immediately.

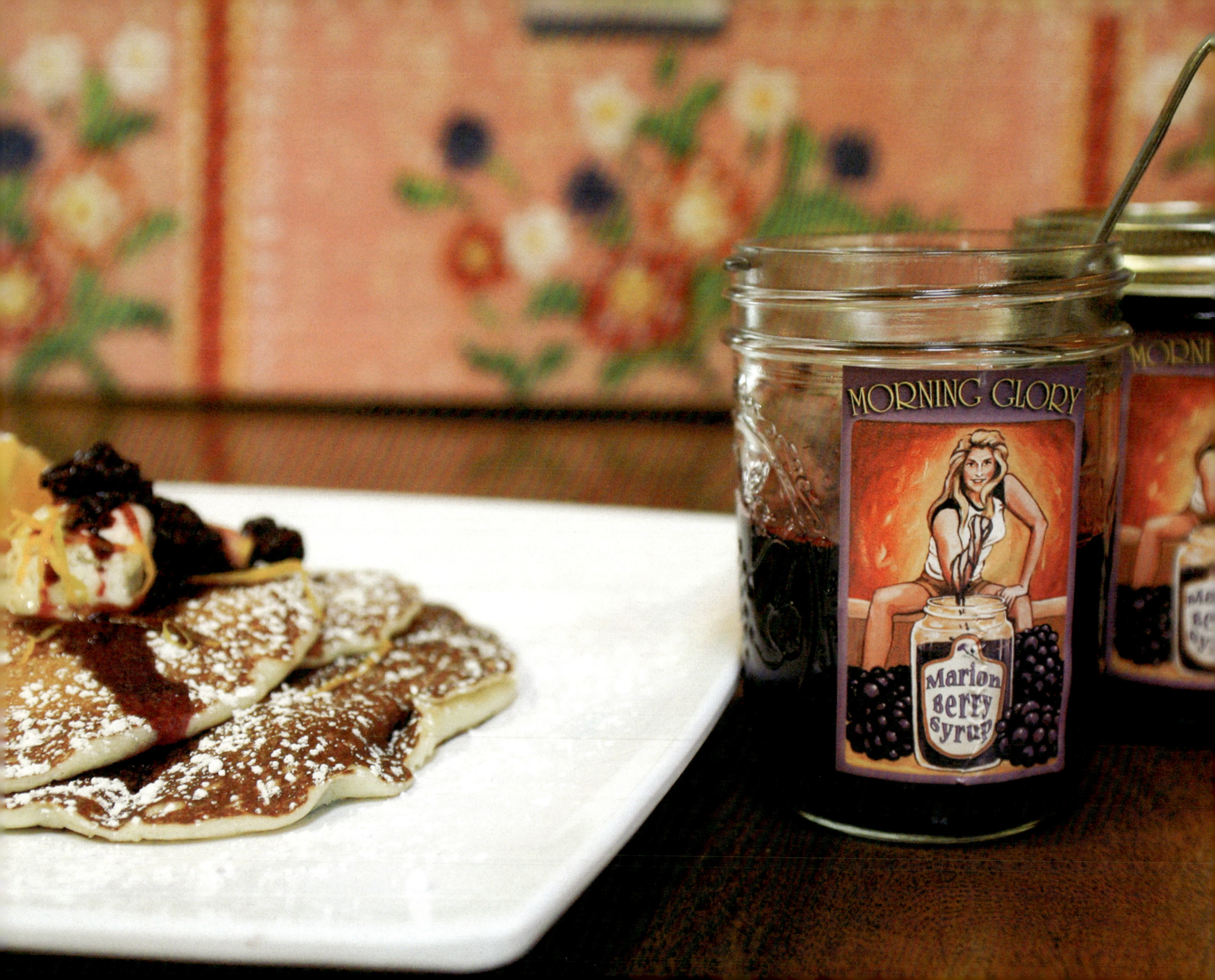
MORNING GLORY
Marion berry syrup

Marionberry Syrup

makes 4 cups

Ingredients

4 cups fresh or frozen marionberries
2 cups sugar
1 Tablespoon lemon juice

Combine in a heavy sauce pan on low heat.
Simmer for 20 minutes.
Chill.

Raspberry Syrup

makes 2 cups

Ingredients

2 cups fresh raspberries
1/2 cup sugar

Pureé raspberries with 1/2 cup sugar. Strain out the seeds.

Make pancakes according to your liking, and top with lemon butter (see recipe in Finishing Touches section), Raspberry Syrup and fresh raspberries.

Dark Cherry Syrup

makes 4 cups

Ingredients

1 12 ounce bag frozen dark cherries
1 13 ounce jar Bonne Maman Cherry Preserves
1 cup sugar
4 cups Knudsen cherry juice
1/2 cup cornstarch

1. In a heavy-bottomed pot, combine the cherries, preserves, sugar and 3 cups of the cherry juice; bring to a simmer.

2. Whisk remaining juice with cornstarch in a separate bowl.

3. Whisk the corn starch/cherry juice mixture into the simmering liquid, lower the heat and simmer, whisking often, for 10 minutes.

Mango Syrup

makes 1 cup

Ingredients

6 fresh mangos
1 cup sugar
1 Tablespoon lemon juice

1. Peel and remove seeds.

2. Dice mango and reserve one cup.

3. In a blender, combine sugar, mango and lemon juice. Blend until smooth.
Fold in diced mango.

Heat to order or serve cold over French toast.

Caramelized Onions

We use these sweet, tangy onions as a condiment in omelets and on sandwiches. They are quite versatile and keep well in the refrigerator for up to two weeks in a covered container, and in the freezer for much longer. The key to their creamy rich texture is cooking them "low and slow" (on low heat, for a long period of time).

makes 3 cups

Ingredients

1 stick butter
1 Tablespoon vegetable oil
2 yellow onions, very thinly sliced
2 red onions, very thinly sliced
1 cup brown sugar
1 cup Balsamic vinegar
Salt and pepper, to taste

1. In a large, heavy-bottomed saucepan, over low heat, melt the butter with the oil.

2. Add the onions, sugar and vinegar. Cook over low heat, stirring occasionally for approximately 1-1/2 hours until translucent and creamy. Season to taste.

Apple Compote

makes 4 cups

Ingredients

2 pounds Granny Smith apples
1 cup brown sugar
1 cup white sugar
1/2 pound of butter
2 Tablespoons vegetable oil
1 teaspoon cinnamon

Peel, core and dice apples. Melt butter and oil in a heavy- bottom pot. Add apples, sugar and cinnamon. cook over low heat for 20 minutes, stirring occasionally.

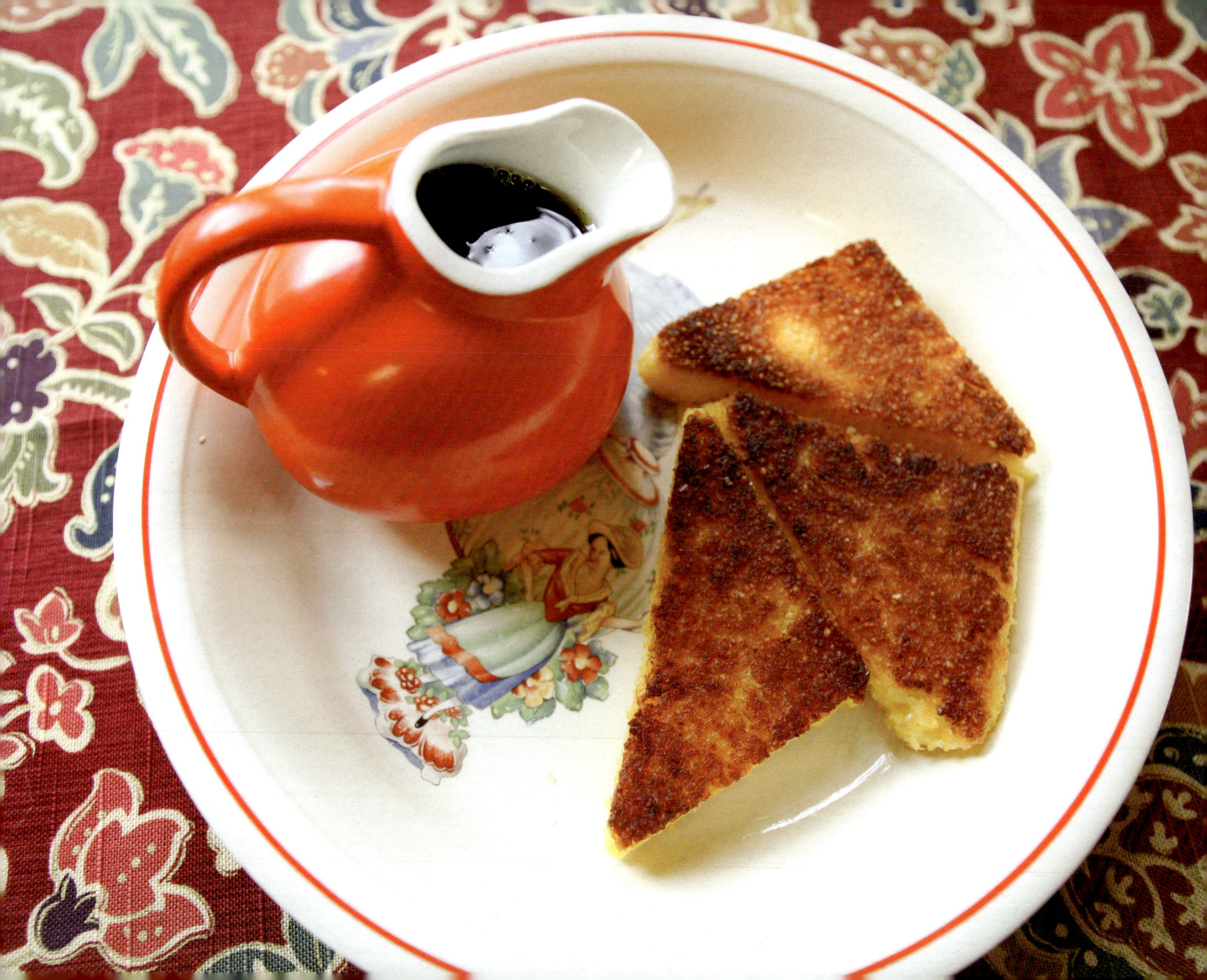

Crispy White Cheddar Polenta

We serve this polenta as a side with our egg dishes. It is crispy on the outside and creamy on the inside. It is also a great side dish for dinner items such as lamb shanks, or layered with Marinara Sauce and Mozzarella.

serves 4

Ingredients

3 1/2 cups water
2 teaspoons salt
1 stick butter
3 cups polenta
1 cup grated white Cheddar
1/2 cup grated Parmesan
2 teaspoons pepper

1. Bring water, salt and butter to a boil.

2. Slowly whisk in polenta. Cook on low heat stirring frequently until thick and creamy, about 20 minutes.

3. Add cheeses and pepper and whisk for 3-4 minutes.

4. Spread onto a sheet tray evenly. You must work quickly as the polenta starts to set up immediately.

5. Refrigerate until firm.

6. Cut into any desired shape and pan fry both sides until golden brown. Serve!

Cheddar Grits

serves 6

Ingredients

2 cups milk
2 cups water
2 cups Quaker "Quick-5 Minute" Grits
(or your favorite brand)
1 cup grated Cheddar cheese
1 teaspoon salt
1 teaspoon pepper

Bring milk and water to a boil. Whisk in grits and lower heat to simmer; continue whisking and cook for five minutes. Season with salt and pepper and stir in Cheddar until melted. Keep warm.

Best career decision ever: Being a Mom

PLEASE JOIN US FOR
ADRIAN'S 1ST TEDDY BEAR PICNIC
BIRTHDAY PARTY

WHEN: SATURDAY, MARCH 5TH

WHERE: ADRIAN'S HOUSE
540 OAK STREET, ASHLAND
RSVP: 488-0191

BEAR TIME: 2:00-5:00

PLEASE BRING YOUR FAVORITE BEAR.

My First Collage was Adrian's invitation.

Giddyup cowboys & cowgirls! Dress up in your favorite duds and come join me by the fire for a birthday celebration. Saddle up at Adrian's corral on Sunday, March 3rd at high noon.

Yippee! I'm 3!

Road Trip: Pre-Morning Glory in a 1956 Rambler

Today's Specials

What is it like to run a restaurant? I read somewhere that line cooking was second only to being an air traffic controller, as the most stressful job. I'm not sure if that is true or not, but I would believe it! There are so many factors involved between the staff, the customers and the actual building itself. I can say, after being in this profession for over 40 years, that it never gets easier. Each day when you walk through the backdoor, you never know what sort of issue you will be facing, but there ALWAYS is one!

> Broken pipes, broken equipment, broken employees, clogged toilets and sinks, fires, injuries, power outages and more
> (I could go on, but I'll stop there)

Employees give you the biggest challenge, of course, because you are relying on everyone to be there and on time. Just having one person call in or not show up can cause absolute chaos. Just having one person missing is like having a broken cog-in-a-wheel. Your employees, become your family and I have been so blessed to have the core staff that I do. We share so much, all of the pain and the joy of life and it is this crew that makes Morning Glory magic.

Morning Glory
Breakfast Lunch Libations

From the kitchen of
Patricia A. Groth

MORNING GLORY

I was now single with a one and a half year old and no source of income. My mother and I, as partners, started purchasing houses in Ashland. I became a self-made contractor and started renovating homes for rentals. I loved the building and designing and it allowed me to bring Adrian with me. I also became the assistant at a local bed and breakfast in Ashland and I remember when I applied for the job that the owner Shirley, said to me "you are over qualified!" and I said "I know, but, I need a job!"

One day, driving down Siskiyou Boulevard, I spotted this little green craftsman style home for sale. Adrian was by now three years old and I felt as though he was old enough that I could conceive of finally opening my own restaurant (boy was I wrong!). In retrospect, if I had known how difficult it would be with a young child, I am not so sure that I would have done it. Of course, I was in uncharted territory. Determined to finally have my own breakfast place, I called my mother and once again, she agreed to finance the new project. The house seemed perfect; quaint, small and right across from SOU.

I found an architect (Tom Giordano) and with him, started to design Morning Glory. I cannot begin to tell you how many people told me that it was the worst location ever! "You need to be on the plaza!" they would say. I didn't want to be "on the plaza!" and continued to overcome the many obstacles ahead of me. Parking was an issue, the width of the driveway was an issue and I had neighbors and other restaurants fighting to keep me from opening. I attended many city council meetings and hearings, until I finally got approval. I have to say that when you believe in your vision and are passionate enough about it, you will prevail.
We could now start building!

From the kitchen of
Patricia A. Groth

MORNING GLORY

It was at this time that tragedy stuck, once again. My mother, my best friend, my confidant and partner passed away unexpectedly. I was beyond devastated and everything came to a grinding halt. The building was halfway done, but the construction could not continue until my mother's estate was settled. The building sat there, and it wasn't until I sold my own home that I was able to move forward. I didn't care at the time anyway, because I could barely cope with my grief. I never felt so alone. It took about 4-5 months for the building to resume and I needed that time to re-group and get focused again. I started to compile a staff and brought back many of my former employees from the McCully house.

I called my good friend Bob Sampson, another CIA classmate, and he came out from Colorado to help me open the restaurant. He was supposed to stay for six weeks and ended up staying for six months! I had to get open and there was still so much to do! Signage, logos, menu design and the actual recipes, some of which, still had to be developed. I was literally writing out recipes on tiny scrapes of paper, up until the day we opened, thinking that I would have time to create a recipe book, in the future. With as much experience that I had already garnered, I was incredibly naïve and overly ambitious when I opened Morning Glory. Housemade hashbrowns? Housemade jam? What was I thinking? We couldn't keep up. The sheer initial volume of customers took me by surprise. The plan was to have a 'soft' opening and to slowly get organized.
Well, that didn't happen. We were surprised that Ashland was so excited to have a new breakfast restaurant, and the fact that I had a following from The McCully House helped. I remember sitting on the back steps just bawling after the first two days, as the stress of it all was finally hitting me.

Marty

Isa

Alejandro   Manuel

Chuy

Omar Rueben Isa

Daniel Gavin Daniella Jade

Tina Micah

Kyle

Cricket

What REALLY Happened That Night...

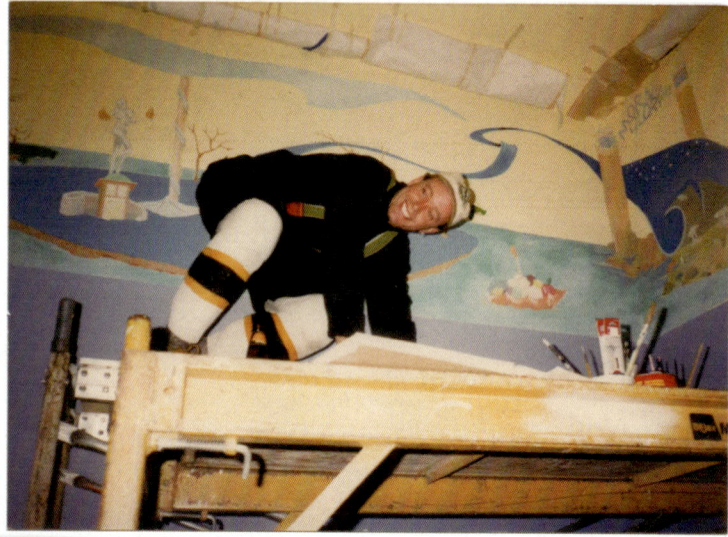

It was 10 pm. I had just gotten in from a long production shoot in Austin, Texas and had prepared the layout for the huge mural on the wall of the yet-to-be Morning Glory Restaurant. My boyfriend at the time, David Fredrickson, who was doing the custom carpentry work for the interior, and his new best friend, Michael Donnelly, introduced me to their friend opening a new restaurant, Patty Groth. She was looking for an artisit. Suddenly, we werein the thick of imaginative, creative, empowered talks about the mood of her restaurant. Her enthusiasm was infectious. Which leads me back to being onan extension ladder at 10pm. I just had to see how the layout I had spent months on in Texas was going to look on the wall.

I can't tell you the sinking feeling that comes over you when you realize you are 18' in the air and the bottom of the extenstion ladder is yes, definitely, sliding out from under you. I can't help but laugh now but that was no fun at the time. Thankfully, (although I didn't think that at the time) in preparation for a sink, there was a pipe sticking out of the wall aobut 5' from the ground. That pipe was just perfectly placed to break the momentum of the plummeting ladder. Unfortunately, the descending ladder, with me on it, sheered the pipe right off and out shot a force of water straight out and across the room. It was flooding quickly. I called David in a panic. He came right over and turned the water off at the water main. The surge was over and the clean up began.

Patty was totally understanding about it and David solved it beautifully and replaced the ladder with full-on scaffolding. I think I got PTSD from the fall because I spent the entirety of the next 3 weeks feeling as though the scaffolding could collapse years, at odd intervals, I would hear from Patty: "Lets put the Basho poem on the wall" or "we are doing a renovation and closing for 3 days, wanna paint on a wall?!" The town of Ashland loves Morning Glory and Patty's generosity of spirit is why. Thanks for inviting me on the ride Patty!!
    -Laney

Every afternoon, I would stop by to see Laney's progress on the mural, and I would always say "That's amazing!" and then the very next day, it would be completely different and I would again say "That's amazing!"
    -Patty.

Laney added more sections over the course of twenty years, which is what you see today.
    -Patty.

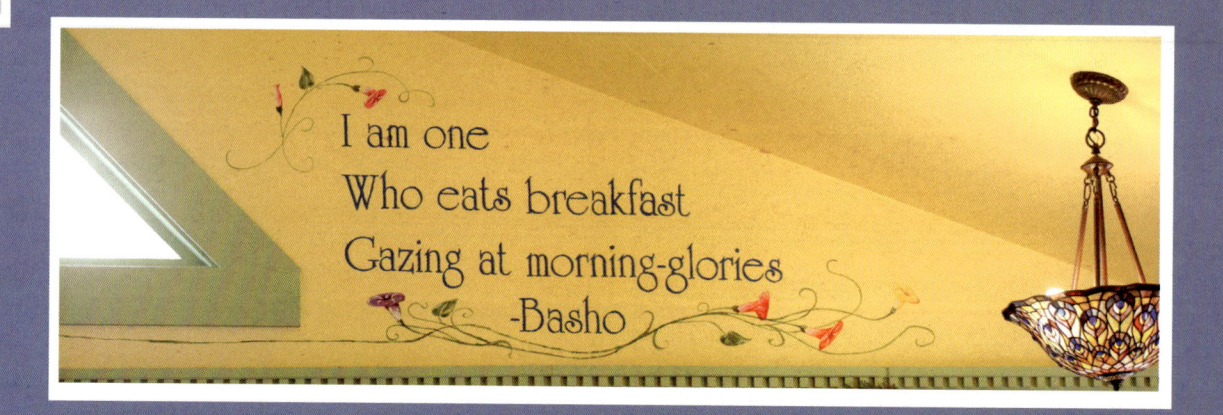

I am one
Who eats breakfast
Gazing at morning-glories
    -Basho

Laney's
Chickens and Fairy Dust

Arwen Knows Where to Find Holiday Cheer

Morning Glory
Open 7 days a week
8am-1:30
1149 Siskiyou Blvd
Ashland, Oregon
541-488-8636

Arwen Hearts Morning Glory

Morning Glory
Open 7 days a week
8am-1:30
1149 Siskiyou Blvd
Ashland, Oregon
541-488-8636

Morning Glory is growing up with Arwen!

Arwen is taking personal time away from Morning Glory
1149 Siskiyou Blvd Ashland, Oregon 541-488-8636

Celebrate Our 21st Anniversary with Arwen!

Come join us on Saturday March 10th from 8am to 1:30 to celebrate our 21st year! We are finally legal!

Come decked out on our deck!
Dance with Arwen like it's 1997!

- 90's theme- dress like its the 90's
- 90's music and dancing!
- Book Signing with Arwen!
  (our darling poster toddler)
- Free Champagne Toast!
- Ice Cream Floats!
- Full New Menu Inside!
- Outdoor Bar!

at Morning Glory
1149 Siskiyou Blvd Ashland, Oregon 541-488-8636

Chris

Tucker
waiting for bacon

THE GREAT FOOD TRUCK ADVENTURE

To be truthful, over the years I have tried to sell the restaurant. Twice. The first time was in 2001, because the pressures of having a young child while operating a busy restaurant, was taking its toll on me. I got an amazing offer in 2001 and ultimately turned it down. What? The same day that I was counteroffering on the sale, a regular customer, who had all of Disney's accounts for graphics, walked in the restaurant with two beautiful rugs with my logo on it, as a gift to me and I lost it. I thought, "what am I doing?" I called my real estate agent the next day and said that the deal was off. What was really crazy about that day, as well, was that I got a phone call on my way to work, from Chip, my line cook, telling me that the ceiling was collapsing in the basement. A rat had chewed through the piping, and the basement was flooding. It didn't matter to me at that point, all I knew at that moment was that I needed to carry on. I wasn't ready to let it go.

The second time I tried to sell, was about five years ago. It was a big story and we were in the news. A lot. So much so, that I stopped taking interviews from TV stations because our customers were freaking out and the information that was being given, was never correct. "You've sold?", "Are you shutting down?"

At the same time, I was looking for something new. I wanted less stress, and I had come across the website of a couple of women in England that serviced a vintage ice cream truck. I wanted something fun.
Did I ever tell you that I started out in ice cream at the age of 15 at Swenson's in Mill Valley?

One evening, while on eBay, I came across a vintage food truck that looked perfect for what I wanted. 55 other people were bidding at the same time, and I thought, "either go big or go home." I placed my bid and went to bed. The next morning, I ran to look at the results and there it was. "You've Won!" That's when I decided to look at the fine print: must pick up in Massachusetts. What? OMG, how am I going to get the truck all the way across the country? I contacted the owner, Dave Delfino and explained my predicament. It was the beginning of summer and I asked him if he wouldn't mind storing it for me while I came up with a plan.

I contacted my good friend, Michael Donnelly, and asked him if he would like to drive the truck across the country with me. I then let Dave know what I was planning and he mentioned that he wished that he could drive across the country! He had never been to the west coast. I was excited about the journey and was able to secure ten days off. I flew to Boston where Dave picked me up and drove me to Plymouth. On the way to the shop where it was parked, I noticed a black lounge chair sitting on the side of the road. When we got to the truck, I slid the side door open to look inside and realized there was only one seat! The driver's seat! Where was I going to put Michael, who was flying in the very next day?

INDEX

N
Nutella Stuffed French Toast 64
Nutty for ever opening a restaurant!

O
Oatmeal Pancakes 38
Omelets,
  Chicken Basil Sausage 78
  Pepper-Seared Tri-Tip 80
  Tomato Basil 78
Omelet 101 77
OMG, we have to shut down and replace the whole sewage line!
Orange Cream Biscuit 30
Orange Blueberry Pancakes 42
Orange Hollandaise Sauce 142
Orange Chipotle Hollandaise Sauce 142

P
Peas, Tandoori Tofu 90
Pancakes:
  Buckwheat Banana 40
  Buttermilk 52
  Orange Blueberry 42
  Pumpkin Oat 48
  Sour Cream 44
  White Chocolate 46
Parmesan Cheese, Tofu Scramble 88
Pecan Waffle, Whole Grain 56
Pepper Jack Cheese, Huevos Rancheros 110
Pesto, Basil, Swiss Chard Scramble 86
Poaching 101
Polenta, White Cheddar 148
Poppyseed, Lemon Waffle 50
Pumpkin Oat Nut Muffins 24
Pumpkin Oat Pancakes 48

R
Rainbow Swiss Chard Scramble 86
Red Onion, Smoked Salmon Scramble 84
Risotto Kale Cakes 104
Remoulade Sauce 140

S
Salsa Fresca, Masa Cakes 102
Sauces;
  Basil Pesto 139
  Chipotle Lime Hollandaise 142
  Fresh Horseradish 137
  Mushroom Gorgonzola 141
  Orange Chipotle Hollandaise 142
  Orange Hollandaise 142
Scone, Sun-Dried Cherry
SHIT! Are you kidding me! What now?
Shrimp Cakes 100
Smoked Chicken and Corn Hash 98
Smoked Mozzarella Cheese, Tomato Basil Omelet 78
Smoked Salmon Scramble 84
Smoked Tomatillo Salsa 134
Smoked Tomato Chutney, Shrimp Cakes 135
Sour Cream Pancakes 44
Spinach,
  Tofu Scramble 90
Sun-Dried Cherry Chutney 138
  Tandoori Tofu 138
Sweet Potato Hash 98
Syrups:
  Dark Cherry 144
  Mango 144
  Marionberry 144
  Raspberry 144

T
Tandoori Tofu Scramble 90
Tech-no Tard, that's me!
The Finishing Touches
"The Morning After" Bloody Mary
Tofu Scramble 88
Tomatillo Sauce 138
T is for Tucker, my most amazing dog! He is our mascot, and knows exactly where to sit to receive treats!

W
Waffle: Buttermilk 52
  Coconut 58
  Gingerbread 54
  Lemon Poppyseed 50
  Whole Grain Pecan 56
Walnut Butter 132
Walnut, Pumpkin Oat Muffin
Whipped Cream
  Blintzes 70
  Gingerbread Waffle 54
White Chocolate Pancakes 46
WTF?
WTH?

Y
Yukon Potatoes,
  Roasted Sweet Potato Hash 96
  Short Rib Hash 92
  Smoked Chicken and Corn Hash 98
  Southwestern Chorizo Hash 94
  Tandoori Tofu Scramble 90
Yes, We are still here!

Z
Zzzzzz...

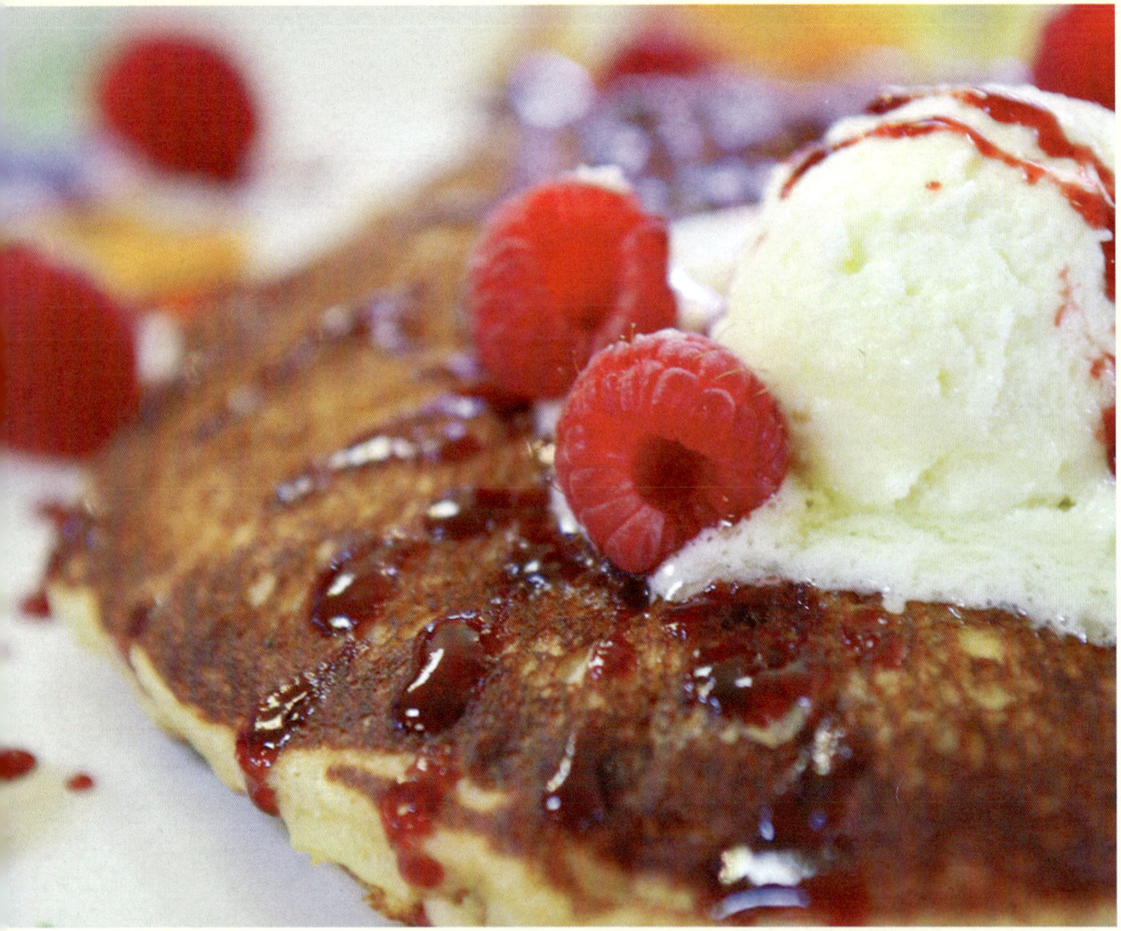

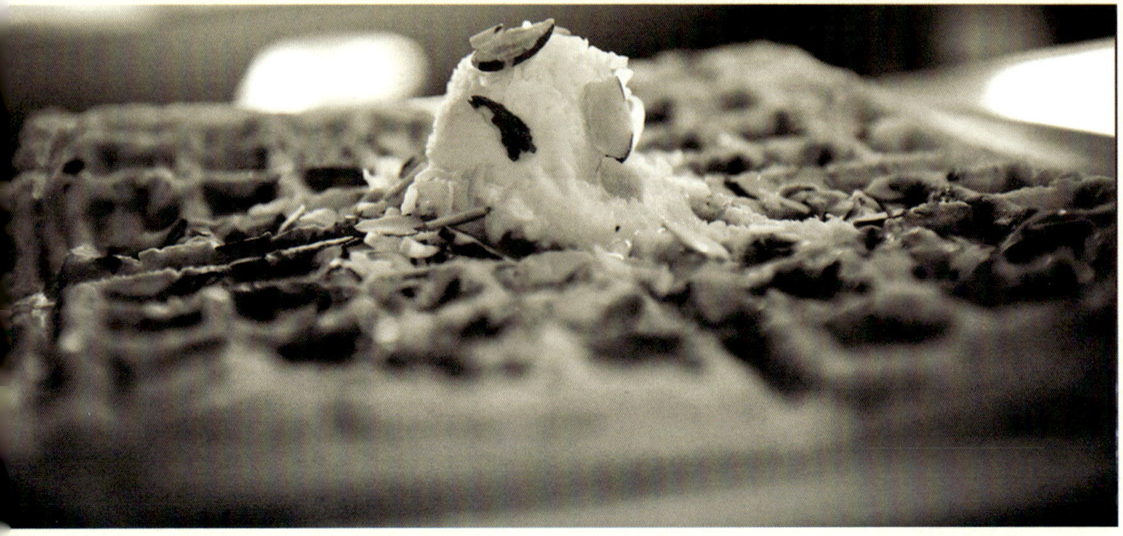

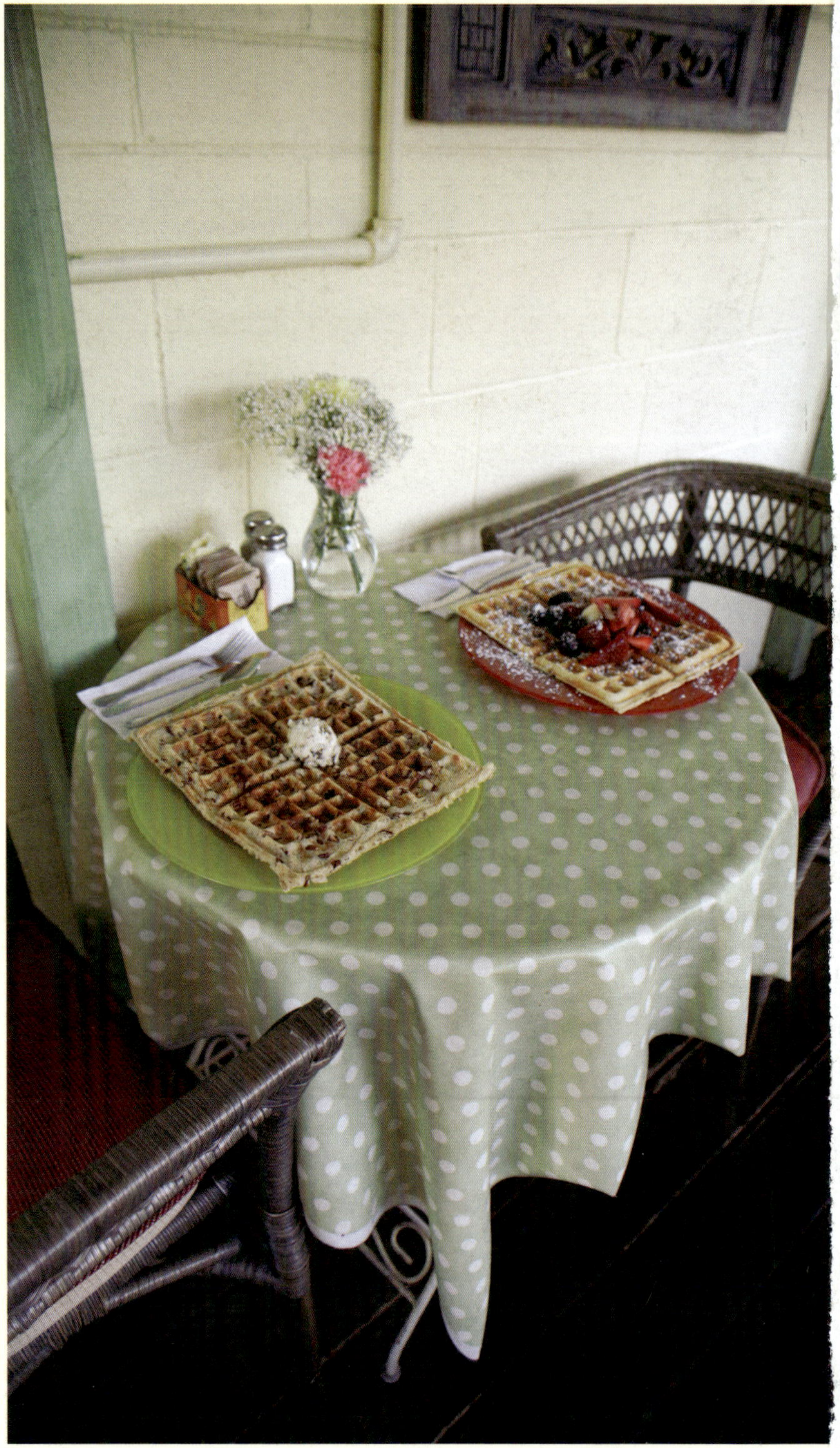

The Magic of Morning Glory
by Diana von Welanetz Wentworth

Award-winning and bestselling cookbook author
and co-author of *Chicken Soup for the Soul Cookbook*

It is 7:45 on a sunny summer morning in the charming, creekside town of Ashland, Oregon. A lively crowd has been gathering in front of a little blue Craftsman-style house on Siskiyou Boulevard anticipating a warm welcome and a memorable meal. My husband Ted and I feel both privileged and a bit sheepish as we bypass the line to enter the back door of what is known as the best breakfast restaurant in the Northwest.

I've been invited to observe and write about the kitchen's morning rush, so Ted settles into a seat at the counter, while I climb onto my assigned perch atop a small square table tucked into the back corner of the kitchen. I enjoy a quick flashback to my favorite pretend game as a child: "short-order cook." Alone in my bedroom, I'd play dual roles of waitress and griddle girl. Jotting down the preferences of imaginary customers on a dime store order pad, I'd hustle over to slap the order on the counter (a bookshelf across the entrance to my little round dressing room) and duck behind, where, surrounded by pretend skillets and a griddle, I'd magically become the cook. How creative and talented I felt preparing three or four breakfast orders at once! I'd yell, "Pick up!" then dash back out to be the waitress and deliver the plates to the families who raved about my delicious food.

Patty Groth, owner/chef of Morning Glory for 21 years, and the "real deal" of my childhood dreams, is now moving to her own beat as she cooks for her crew of helpers and servers, assuring they are cared for first. Breaking eggs over a skillet of barely simmering water, she acknowledges my presence saying, "Some restaurants won't poach eggs! What? They can't boil water?" Using a slotted spoon she lifts out the perfectly poached eggs and places them atop Black Forest Ham on Orange Cream Biscuits. Spooning warm Hollandaise over them, she slides the plated dishes onto the pass-through and calls out to the server. "Bev's comin' up!" Bev appears in a flash to deliver the plates within seconds.

When the front door opens at eight, it takes only minutes to seat seventy customers. And for seventy breakfast orders to be stacked on the pass-through from the dining room.

Chip, this morning's line cook, mans the griddle, forming ovals of hash browns to crisp, ladling thick batter into old-fashioned waffle irons. Patty, herself, masters every omelet; poaches, fries and scrambles every egg. Her passion and high spirits are contagious.

From the kitchen of
Patricia A. Groth

Morning Glory

Introduction:

When I opened the doors of Morning Glory, on that fateful day in March of 1997, little did I know the phenomenon it would become. Morning Glory began with the name, although the concept and the training had been going on for over 20 years. I was not the one to come up with the name, an unknown waiter did.

I was dining out one evening with friends in Ashland and the year was 1995. I had moved to the Rogue Valley in 1989, from the bay area, to open the McCully House Inn in Jacksonville, Oregon which I ran successfully with my partner, Phil Accetta for five years.

After the sale, I took time out to have my son Adrian and moved to nearby Ashland. So here I was, two years later, single, with a two-year-old and ready to start my next project, a restaurant specializing in breakfast.

Back to the name: Morning Glory. A group of us were enjoying dinner on a patio when, out of the blue, a girlfriend who knew of my restaurant plans asked our waiter: "What would you name a famous breakfast restaurant?" He did not even hesitate when he replied "Morning Glory". "That's it", I thought! I had no money and no location, but at least now I had a name!

Here we are twenty-one years later, and it boggles my mind the sheer volume of what my crew and myself have accomplished. Morning Glory is not just a restaurant, it truly is a beloved part of a community that has made it, it's own. Within the pages of your favorite recipes, you will find a story. It is my story, but it is also our story. I hope to give you a sense of what it is like to manage such a special place, and to share with you the joys, successes, and the failures!

So kick up your feet and dive in!

With Love,
Patty Groth

My Mom's cousin Carl, Pat and Bill at Sam's in Tiburon, California. 1963.

dedication

This book is dedicated to my parents Pat and Bill Groth. I would not be where I am today without your love and support. Thanks Mom, for believing in me.

Breakfast at Morning Glory

Recipes, Mishaps and Adventures from the Little Blue House

by Patty Groth

Foreword by award-winning and bestselling cookbook author
Diana von Welanetz Wentworth
Co-Author of the *Chicken Soup for the Soul Cookbook*